Computer Assisted
Home Energy Management

by Paul E. Field

Howard W. Sams & Co., Inc.
4300 WEST 62ND ST. INDIANAPOLIS, INDIANA 46268 USA

Copyright © 1982 by Paul E. Field

FIRST EDITION
FIRST PRINTING—1982

International Standard Book Number: 0-672-21817-8
Library of Congress Catalog Card Number: 82-50649

Edited by: *Jim Rounds*
Illustrated by: *Wm. D. Basham*

Printed in the United States of America.

Preface

The objectives of this book are:
1. To illustrate the fundamentals of the exciting area of micro-computer interfacing;
2. To demonstrate a practical energy monitoring system for performing computer assisted physical measurements;
3. To elaborate the methods of computerized data analysis.

In the process of working through these pages, you will learn these tools of the trade and have a working energy monitor for your home. Although the project can be completed in "cookbook" fashion by following the recipes for the electronic hardware and the programming software, it is hoped that it will encourage you to seek out more information from other sources and launch a fascinating and worthwhile hobby.

Although the specific details of the project are made with reference to the Radio Shack TRS-80® 16K Model I computer, users of other computers can adapt the BASIC programs, machine language routines, and hardware with modest additional effort. The amount of effort depends on how similar your computer is to the TRS-80. It is assumed that the computer has a typewriter keyboard, a video display, cassette tape recorder, and uses the BASIC language for programming. Neither a printer nor a disk operating system is required. In fact, if there is a disk system and it cannot be disabled, then extra effort will be necessary. The only other limitation is that the machine language routines to be described are for members of the 80 family microprocessors:

8080, 8085, Z80, and NSC800. These routines have been documented well enough (including detailed flowcharts) that they can be translated by anyone conversant in one of the other microprocessors' codes.

Events of the past few years indicate that the overindulgence of the past twenty-five year energy usage of our society has ended. Cheap energy is now history and conservation is not only the responsible choice, it has become the only economically viable option. With a personal computer, you can install an energy monitoring system without sacrificing any of the other conveniences of owning a computer. The system described in this book is as inexpensive as possible while still providing all the data necessary to evaluate the performance of your home as an energy consuming system. It is sufficiently versatile that it can be adapted to measure practically any form of energy consumption, not just those specifically described. Half the fun of microcomputer interfacing is being innovative and finding creative ways to solve problems that interest you.

Whatever the long range objectives of this book, the immediate goal is to provide you with sufficient details on the design, construction, and operation of a residential energy monitoring system. Specifically, the system hardware consists of a buffered microcomputer interface, an interrupt driven time-of-day clock, and a thermometer port which measures eight individual temperatures. Listings of five BASIC programs are given along with a thorough discussion of each program. These include a loader of the machine language monitor, a thermometer calibration program with experimental data acquisition and processing, a nine option program of time and temperature data management and summaries, a residential heat loss calculator based on the size and construction parameters of the house, and a statistical analysis program for evaluating the performance characteristics of the home as an energy system.

We start in Chapter 1 with an overview of the important concepts relating to microprocessors, microcomputers, and input/output ports. The next chapter surveys the practical aspects of measuring temperature and time with a microcomputer. A very inexpensive and novel thermometer device is described. Chapter 3 is a description of the design and construction details of all the circuitry required. The circuit is wire-wrapped on a single standard board but has the capability of expansion for additional projects to other boards through a common-bus edge connector. Chapters 4 and 5 cover the machine language program and the BASIC utility programs for the system. These are followed in Chapter 6 with a description of the details and sample calculations of a program to evaluate the heat losses of a residence. This program provides you with information that is useful of itself and also can be compared with data obtained from the monitor. Chapter 7 describes the statistical analysis program and discusses how it can be adapted for general least square analysis of any set of data. Finally, a postscript in Chapter 8 describes variations and refinements you might consider for the completed system.

The author thanks the Blacksburg Group for their encouragement and support. I also acknowledge my brothers and sister-in-law for the practical information they provided for Chapter 6. This book is dedicated to my family: especially to my mother who worked at a retail coal business after the premature death of my father so that we could make it; to my sister, who was my counsel in youth; to Jewell, who has been my counsel since; and to Sylvia, Randy, and Thom, who must live in a society more energy conscious than ours has been.

PAUL E. FIELD

Contents

Interfacing Fundamentals

Chapter 1 —————————————————————————

This chapter is a brief survey of the fundamentals of microcomputer interfacing. It is not intended to be exhaustive. It is written to serve as an overview for readers with some familiarity with digital electronics in an effort to introduce and review the basic concepts and terminology of microcomputer interfacing. Experienced readers may need only to scan this chapter. It is hoped that readers with little or no knowledge of digital electronics and microprocessors will find this a useful introduction that may ease their initiation into the subject. In any event, we conclude the chapter with suggestions for further reading.

All microprocessors have three essential elements that they need to communicate with the external world. Since we will be dealing with microprocessor-based home computers, our particular interests will concentrate on how these three elements function in the microcomputer. Each of these elements answers one of the questions: What?, Where?, and When? The three elements are:

1. an 8-bit bidirectional Data Bus
2. a 16-bit Address Bus, and
3. various control signals we will collectively refer to as the Control Bus.

These are illustrated in Fig. 1-1. We define a bus as a collection of wire connections used either to send or to receive digital information between the microprocessor and any other devices that communicate with the microprocessor. By digital information we mean electrical signals which, at a specific moment, are either at the voltage supply level, typically +5 V known as "logic 1," or at ground potential, that is zero volts and known as "logic 0." An 8-bit bus therefore consists of eight lines (or wires), each of which at any moment will have either a logic 1 (+ 5 V) or a logic 0 (0 V). Each signal thus represents a binary digit (bit).

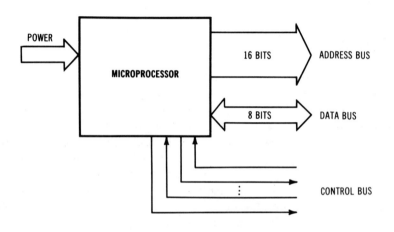

Figure 1-1
Bus structure of a microprocessor.

In referring to the 8-bit data bus, we noted that it was bidirectional. This means that signals may be transmitted in either direction over the lines in the bus. The convention for specifying which direction the data travels is always made with reference to the microprocessor. Input signals are those that flow *from* an external device *into* the microprocessor. Output signals flow *out* of the microprocessor *to* external devices. Thus, the data bus can carry both input and output signals. The data bus, as its name implies, carries the data signals. It answers the question What? Data is any numeric information that the microprocessor can manipulate. It may represent the whole or partial value of some measurement or, as we shall see later, it may be coded information which the microprocessor uses to carry out a particular task. Since we are considering an 8-bit data bus, there are only 256 possible binary (base 2) combinations of 1s and 0s that can be obtained from a signal transmitted as eight parallel bits. The decimal (base 10) range of these numbers is 0 to 255. Not to 256! (since the number zero gets counted as a legitimate value). Any set of eight bits is conventionally referred to as a *byte*. Thus, one data byte represents a number between 0 and 255.

The address bus consists of 16 bits (or lines or wires). It is an output bus and, as such, only carries information in the form of 16 binary digits from the microprocessor to external devices. Since it consists of two bytes of information, it represents 256 × 256 or 65,536 possible values ranging from 0 to 65,535. (Remember that zero gets counted.) The address bus answers the question Where? It is used by the microprocessor to determine from or to which external device the data (What?) is to be transmitted.

The majority of external devices that a microprocessor has to deal with are memory registers. A register is simply a device that can retain (hold or remember) digital information. There are registers which can hold only one bit (called a data latch) and there are registers which can hold many bits of digital information. Since we are considering 8-bit microprocessors, then the memory registers should logically be 8-bit registers. A memory register is alternatively referred to as a memory location. Each memory location has a unique address so that when the microprocessor specifies "Where," the data are transmitted only to (or from) that register. Applying the direction convention to memory, to input data from memory to the microprocessor is referred to as a "read" operation and to output data from the microprocessor to memory is referred to as a "write" operation. Although a microcomputer may have a maximum of 65,536 memory locations, most operate with considerably less. As an aside, we might note that because ten bits of information represents 1024 possible values and the conventional abbreviation for 1000 is K (kilo-), usage has come to denote K for 1024 in computer terminology. Thus 65,536 which equals 64 × 1024 is referred to as 64K. Table 1-1 lists the various common sizes that are derived from the binary number system.

One reason that many computers are not used with a full 64K of memory locations is that a certain number of register addresses are set aside for external devices that are wired to appear to the

Table 1–1. Binary Number Sizes

Power	Number	Denotation
2^0	1	bit
2^1	2	- (binary base)
2^2	4	-
2^3	8	byte (octal base)
2^4	16	- (hexadecimal base)
2^5	32	
2^6	64	
2^7	128	
2^8	256	page
2^9	512	1/2K
2^{10}	1024	1K
2^{11}	2048	2K
2^{12}	4096	4K
2^{13}	8192	8K
2^{14}	16384	16K
2^{15}	32768	32K
2^{16}	65536	64K

microprocessor as memory registers. This technique is called memory-mapped I/O (input/output) to distinguish it from memory read/write. We might note here another convention used in computer terminology. An external device that is not a memory register is usually referred to as a port (input and/or output). In a similar manner, the words "read" and "write" are used to reference memory registers while the words "input" and "output" are used to reference I/O ports.

One family of microprocessors consisting of the 8080, 8085, and Z80 uses a second technique for communicating with external devices other than memory registers. In this method, the data is transferred between the Accumulator register of the micro-processor and the device. This method is referred to as Accumulator I/O to distinguish it from memory-mapped I/O. Each port still requires a unique address; however, only an 8-bit address is used. This obviously limits the number of port addresses to 256. Bear in mind that these I/O addresses are in addition to those that might be used with memory-mapped I/O.

The 8-bit address for Accumulator I/O is obtained from half of the address bus. To distinguish the 16 lines in the address bus they are labeled A15, A14, . . . A1, A0. A15 represents the most significant bit (leftmost binary digit) and distinguishes the higher 32K locations from the lower 32K. A0 is the least significant bit (rightmost digit) and distinguishes adjacent locations as odd or even. Since the address bus forms two bytes we make the further distinction of lines A15-A8 as the high address and lines A7-A0 as the low address. Without going into the differences of the 80 family microprocessors, we can observe here that the low address bus will carry the 8-bit address that is necessary to define uniquely a port for Accumulator I/O.

We now come to the third element essential to the operation of a computer. This is the control bus, the various signals of which answer the question When? Actually, it might be more appropriate to say that the lines of the control bus answer both How and When? We should start by observing that the major differences between all microprocessors are really in the number and kind of control signals they use. Even members of the same family use different signals and methods for implementing control of external devices.

The basic function of the control lines is to coordinate and synchronize the timing of the microprocessor with those devices connected to the data and address buses. This is the answer to the question When? We have already noted that the 80 family microprocessors have two different ways in which they use the address bus to select memory registers or I/O ports. There are control lines that make this distinction to answer the question How?

Of the many different control lines that make up the control bus, some are input signals and some are output signals. We shall limit our attention to the six controls of particular importance to microcomputer interfacing. These are the input (IN*), output (OUT*), memory read (RD*), memory write (WR*), interrupt request (INT*), and interrupt acknowledge (INTA*) signals. All six lines are indicated with asterisks over their labels to indicate that their active state is a logic 0. This means that the inactive or quiescent state is a logic 1 or + 5 V. Recognizing the names of the first four controls listed should make clear how the decision is made whether the entire 16 lines of the address bus should be used for memory register operations or whether the lower 8 address lines are to be used for I/O port operation. Memory chips are wired to the RD* and WR* control lines whereas Accumulator I/O devices are connected to the IN* or OUT* control lines. It should also be apparent that the direction of data flow on the data bus is selected by one or the other of each of these pairs of control signals.

It must be emphasized that each memory location and I/O port must respond to a unique address. Usually this means that the address bus must be decoded such that the 16 (or 8) address bits are combined using digital logic devices (decoders) to create a single pulse that is used to select (enable) the specific device. In working with I/O devices (also called peripheral devices), this single pulse is referred to as the "device code." Typically, this device code is then combined (using digital logic) with the appropriate control pulse (IN* or OUT*) to create a pulse called the "device select pulse" (DSP). It is the DSP that actually makes a device respond to the microprocessor.

The remaining two control lines (INT* and INTA*) are also used to answer the question How? but by an approach that differs significantly from our previous discussion. Up to now we have considered interfaced devices always to be under the control of the microprocessor. They were expected to be ready either to send or to receive data when the microprocessor was ready. The interrupt (INT*) and interrupt acknowledge (INTA*) control signals permit peripheral devices literally to interrupt the microprocessor while it is performing some other task. This is usually the case when the peripheral device needs immediate service to operate properly and cannot wait for the micro-processor to get to that part of its program that services the device.

The INT* is an active low input to the microprocessor, which means that the line is ordinarily at +5 V and that it is activated by a short ground (0 V) pulse. An INTA* is an active low output signal sent by the microprocessor shortly after receipt of an INT* request. It is not transmitted until the microprocessor has completed whatever bookkeeping that needs to be done before it can service the interrupting device. This bookkeeping includes completing the machine language instruction it was performing at the time of the interrupt request and also of saving its place in its program. The value of the interrupt acknowledge signal is that it can be used to trigger the interrupting device to proceed to interact with the microprocessor. In this respect, it is similar to the input, output, read, and write control signals. It can also be used to reset the interrupt signal originated by the peripheral device.

There are several methods of interrupt servicing. Generally the different types of microprocessors use one or more of these methods. Broadly, interrupt service can be classified into three types:

1. single-line interrupt
2. multilevel interrupts
3. vectored interrupts.

The important distinction between the three cases is the method used to direct the microprocessor to the memory address which stores the first instruction of a program to service the interrupt. A second distinction is the number of lines physically available on the microprocessor. In the case of single-line and multilevel interrupts, the memory address for the service routine (program) is internally programmed into the microprocessor. Multilevel interrupts are simply several single-level interrupt control lines on the same microprocessor; there are three on the 8085. For vectored interrupt service, the interrupting device must place an instruction on the data bus that directs (vectors) the microprocessor to one of several (typically eight) possible starting addresses. This instruction is usually one of the Restart commands which function as one-byte subroutine Call instructions. For all 80 family microprocessors, the INT* control input operates as a vector interrupt control. It is possible by either hardware (external circuitry) or software (in the case of the Z80) to make the vectored interrupt line operate as a single-line interrupt. We might also note that for a microprocessor to have only one (single-line) interrupt does not mean that there can only be one interrupting device. By use of software, a technique known as polling can be implemented in which several devices can trigger the interrupt request line and the first part of the service routine consists of determining which device made the request. We shall consider more about interrupt service in Chapter 3.

Throughout this discussion we have been careful to make reference to the microprocessor per se with little specific mention of the microcomputer being made. A microprocessor requires at least three additional components in order to function as a microcomputer. First, it obviously needs some memory registers to store both the operating program (instruction sequence) and data. Second, it would be a totally useless object if it did not include an input device and an output device. Although I/O devices may be as elementary as a set of switches for input and a set of lamps for output, we shall assume the configuration of a typewriter keyboard and a video display more typically found in personal computers. Third, the microcomputer must have all the associated digital logic circuitry necessary to coordinate its memory and I/O. Finally, although not an absolute necessity, it is highly desirable that the microcomputer be equipped with a high-level language (such as BASIC) to make its operation simple. Fig. 1-2 illustrates the components of a microcomputer.

Of greatest importance to the interfacer, given the preceding minimum requirements for a microcomputer, is the availability of, and easy access to, the address, data, and control buses. As we have seen, this means that whatever else may be contained within the microcomputer, there has to be a bus connector consisting of some 30 lines available for interfacing.

There are several practical aspects of interfacing that should be reviewed. The most important of these is that signals from two or more devices cannot be connected to a single input line of another device. The reason becomes apparent when one considers the case in which one device is trying to set a logic 1 by maintaining + 5 V on the line, while a second device is trying to set a logic 0 by maintaining 0 V on the same line. The current sourcing (+ 5 V) device will exceed its current handling capability when it sees a direct line to ground and most likely burn out. Up to this point we have implied that up to 256 input devices can be wired in parallel on the data bus. This is true with one very important provision: namely that only one device may be active at any given moment. When one device is active and attempting to place information on

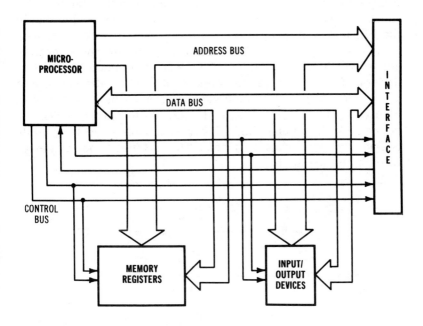

Figure 1-2
Components of a microprocessor.

the data bus, all the other devices must appear to be disconnected, that is, they should have such a high impedance (resistance) that they neither attempt to sink or source any current from the active device.

The solution to this problem is solved by using tristate digital devices at the data outputs of each input port. As its name implies, a tristate device has three possible states: a logic 1, a logic 0, and a high impedance state. Such devices require a digital control signal in order to be enabled so that they are no longer in the high impedance state. As long as the enable input is active, the outputs of the device are active and transmit their logic state values of 0 or 1. As soon as the enable input becomes inactive the device output lines go into their high impedance state. Typically, the signals from the input device are connected to tristate drivers (buffers or inverters) the outputs of which are then connected in parallel with the other devices sharing the data bus. There are many tristate integrated circuit (IC) devices available for interfacing. The schematic representation of tristate drivers is shown in Fig. 1-3. In the TTL family of integrated circuits, the enable input of a tristate device is usually active low, although there are some that are active high. Table 1-2 lists a few of the more common TTL tristate drivers. The enable input controls of tristate drivers are of particular value to microcomputer interfacing because they can be used by the microprocessor to activate the input device. By connecting the unique DSP (device select pulse) to the tristate enable of an input port, only one input device at a time can place its data on the data bus.

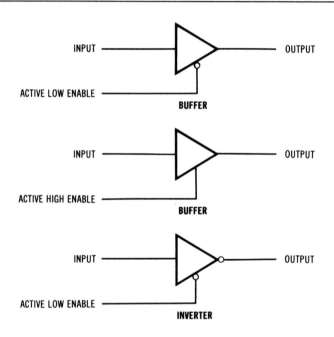

Figure 1-3
A tristate driver schematic.

A second practical aspect of interfacing concerns output ports that receive data from the microprocessor. This is not the same problem just encountered with input devices, because within the current driving limits of the devices, it is quite acceptable to have

Table 1-2. TTL Three-State Drivers

Series Number	Driver Type	Enable Logic	Number of Drivers/IC	Number of Enables	Drivers/ Enable
74125	BUFFER	0	4	4	1
74126	BUFFER	1	4	4	1
74240	INVERTER	0	8	2	4
74244	BUFFER	0	8	2	4
74365	BUFFER	0	6	2	6
74366	INVERTER	0	6	2	6
74367	BUFFER	0	6	2	4,2
74368	INVERTER	0	6	2	4,2

one output connected to as many inputs as it can drive. In fact, since the outputs of the microprocessor IC chip can usually only drive slightly more than one standard TTL load (1.6 mA), the outputs of the microprocessor are generally directly connected to line drivers. This enhances the current driving capacity up to ten standard TTL loads.

The problem with output devices is one concerning the duration of the data being supplied by the microprocessor. For a microprocessor operating at 2 MHz, the data is only present for 0.5 microsecond. If the output device requires the data for a longer time than this, it must retain the data after it is no longer present on the data bus. Therefore, when interfacing output devices, it is usual to employ eight data latches to receive and hold the data until it is replaced by the next byte transmitted from the microprocessor to the port. Probably the most common data latches used in interfacing output ports are the 7474 and 7475 (TTL family). The differences between these two types of ICs illustrate some of the important considerations that have to be made in designing an output port interface.

Each latch on both the 7474 and the 7475 provides complementary outputs, Q and Q*, has a data input, D, and an enable input. The enable is usually called a clock, CLK, input. The 7474 is a 14-pin IC containing two completely independent latches having, in addition, a Preset input, PR, which sets Q to a logic 1 (Q* = 0), and a Clear input, CLR, which resets Q to a logic 0 (Q* = 1). The 7475 is a 16-pin IC and contains four data latches and two clock inputs with two latches sharing one clock input. It does not have the overriding preset and clear inputs. The most significant difference between the 7474 and 7475 ICs is the way the clock signal causes the data to be transferred from D to the Q and Q* outputs. This is most easily understood by first realizing that the trigger pulse sent to the clock input is active high. This means that the quiescent state of the clock is at 0 V. With the generation of the pulse, the voltage rises from 0 V to +5 V and forms the rising (positive) edge of the pulse. The clock pulse stays at the logic 1 level until it is complete and then returns to the logic 0 level. In returning to 0 V, the trailing (negative) edge of the pulse is formed. The 7474 is a positive edge triggered latch which means that the state of the D input is passed to the Q output on the rising edge of the clock pulse and latched. Since no further latching action can occur until the next positive (rising) edge, the device is not dependent on the duration of the pulse. In contrast to the 7474, the 7475 is level triggered which means that once the pulse is at a logic 1, the state at the D input is passed to the Q output. However, in this case, the output is latched on the negative (trailing) edge of the clock pulse. Thus, if D should change states during the time the clock pulse is high, then Q will follow D and change accordingly. For this reason, the 7475 is referred to as a "follower" latch.

One final practical aspect of microcomputer interfacing concerns the current driving capacities of the signals found at the interface connector. It is NOT good practice to assume that these signals can drive more than one regular TTL load. When you are designing an interface, your first step should be to buffer all signals. In this way, you can be certain of the current driving capacities of the output signals and also be assured that the input signals from the interface to the microcomputer can sink and source enough current to be transmitted through the long lengths of cable used to connect the microcomputer and the interface circuitry.

There is much more that could be said about the characteristics of microprocessors, the variety of digital logic devices, and the design of interfaces. However, most of this is beyond the scope of this book. As we stated at the outset, our interest shall be directed towards developing a residential energy management system that will utilize the attributes of a home computer. To help you seek further details on interfacing topics, the books listed in the final paragraph of this chapter are recommended for further reference.

To summarize the most important aspects of microcomputer interfacing, you should understand and be able to explain the significance of the following five concepts:

1. The difference between memory-mapped I/O and Accumulator I/O
2. The concept of address bus decoding to create a unique device code.
3. The method of creating a Device Select pulse (DSP).
4. The importance of three-state buffering of input devices on the data bus and control bus input lines.
5. The need for latching data bus information for output ports.

Suggested titles for further reading on digital electronics and microcomputer programming and interfacing can be found in the *Blacksburg Continuing Education Series* published by Howard W. Sams & Co., Inc. The approach of this series is very practical and straightforward. You would be best advised to scan the individual books to find those appropriate to your interests and level of understanding. The one valuable book that the author recommends without qualification is *TRS-80 Interfacing, Book 2* (Titus, Titus, and Larsen, 1980). This book is an excellent summary of personal computer interfacing concepts.

Measuring Temperature

If you want to manage your home's energy consumption, the first thing you have to know is how much energy you are using and where you are using it. Of course, it is possible to analyze your energy consumption based on your fuel, electric, and other energy bills, but they only give the total expenditures. The total expenditure needs to be divided into subtotals that can be more readily managed. The two largest expenditures of the average home energy bill go for space heating and for domestic hot water consumption for the kitchen and bath.

Degree Days

Because the amount of fuel used in a home depends on how cold it is outside over a period of time, some method for determining this quantity is required. Fortunately, a method exists that is simple and amazingly accurate. This method is based on calculating a quantity, called a "degree day," which measures the number of degrees difference between a standard temperature (usually) of 65°F and the average outdoor temperature over a 24-hour period. For example, if the high temperature for a particular day was 60 and the low temperature for that day was 20, then the average temperature was 40 and the number of degree days is 65 – 40 or 25 for that day. In equation form, the number of degree days per day is calculated as:

$$DD = 65 - \left(\frac{T_{high} + T_{low}}{2} \right)$$

Note that we are dealing in temperatures on the Fahrenheit scale. The reference temperature of 65°F is based on the fact that homes usually do not consume any fuel for space heating when the average daily temperature is 65° or above. Strictly speaking, we have defined the "heating degree day." When the average temperature is above 65° a negative number would be calculated that is a useless value for heating calculations. For this reason, any day that has an average temperature greater than 65° is recorded as having zero degree days. Sometimes these negative values are recorded (without the minus sign) as "cooling degree days" and are used in summer cooling calculations.

The U.S. Weather Service keeps daily records of the number of degree days at their various observation stations, such as at metropolitan airports. These values are often published in city newspapers under the weather information by listing both the number of degree days for the previous day and the total number for the current heating season. The usual heating season begins on July 1 and runs to June 30 of the following year.

Various high-low thermometers can be purchased for manually keeping daily records. However, this is one area where the home computer can perform the job at a modest cost and provide a very useful service. The prospect of having a computer keep these records as well as performing some additional information gathering tasks on distribution of energy consumption is the whole purpose of this book.

Time Measurements

There are four kinds of information we will want to acquire. First, we will want to be able to determine the outdoor temperature periodically and keep a record of the highest and lowest observed temperatures. This will provide the data needed to calculate the number of degree days for each 24-hour period and evaluate the "heat load" required. Second, we will want to monitor the distribution of heat to the various sections (zones) of the house. Third, we will want to monitor the distribution and consumption of domestic hot water. Fourth, it will be useful to keep a record on the operating time of the heat plant.

It is obvious that all four sets of data are dependent on being able to determine the time. If the computer is to monitor the outdoor temperature periodically and also keep a 24-hour record, it is clear that a time-of-day clock will have to be included in the system. The latter three classes of data are, in fact, time measurements. That is, in monitoring distribution and consumption, the simplest quantity to evaluate is how much time a particular device is active, or "on." For these "time-on" measurements, we can determine when the device is active by sensing its temperature. If the temperature is above a certain value, called the "set point," the device is on, and when the temperature is below the set-point temperature, the device is off. The computer has only to keep a record of the total time on for a given period.

Measuring time is a relatively easy task and can be implemented by interfacing an integrated clock circuit. We shall consider these details in subsequent chapters on hardware and software.

Temperature Measurement

The important and practical question that needs to be considered now is how can many different temperatures be monitored inexpensively? There are many types of devices that convert temperature into an electrical signal which can be processed by the computer. Most can be categorized into one of three classes determined by the electrical property which is dependent on the temperature. These properties are voltage, resistance, and current. Table 2-1 summarizes a few of the most common thermometer devices.

Table 2-1. Electrical Thermometers

Type	Electrical Property	Temperature Coefficient
Thermocouple	Voltage	0.04 mV/deg.(Type K)
Resistance Thermometer	Resistance	0.3 ohm/deg.(Platinum)
Thermistor	Resistance	−5%/deg.
Semiconductor Junction	Current	1 μamp/deg.(AD590)

No device is perfectly linear in temperature. That is, the change in property per degree change in temperature is not the same for all temperatures over the range that the device operates. This is even true for the common liquid in glass thermometers in which the property being measured is actually the volume change of the liquid (alcohol, mercury, etc.). In all but the most precise work, the small differences that result from nonlinearity are not of any consequence over the relatively small temperature ranges of usual interest, say between the freezing point and boiling point of water.

Thermistors

A glaring example of nonlinear temperature dependence is seen in the case of thermistors. In Table 2-1, the temperature coefficient is given as a percentage change. For example, if the thermistor has a resistance of 10,000 ohms at 25°C (77°F), then its resistance will decrease by 9500 ohms at 26°; that is: 10000 × (1 − 0.05) = 9500. Note that the coefficient is negative and that the resistance decreases as the temperature increases. At 27°C, the resistance will drop another 5% of the value at 26° to become 9500 − 475 = 9025 ohms. Any quantity that changes by a percentage of its value instead of by an absolute amount is logarithmic in nature. Probably the most common example of logarithmic behavior is the manner in which financial interest is compounded. For example, the manner in which mortgage payments are divided between the interest payment and the reduction of the principal is governed by the same mathematical relationship as that which applies to a thermistor.

Writing the algebraic expression in terms of the thermistor, the equation is:

$$R(T) = R(0) \times (1 - C) \uparrow (T - T(0))$$

where,
R(T) is the thermistor resistance at the temperature of interest, T,
R(0) is the thermistor resistor at some specified reference temperature, say 25°C,
C is the temperature coefficient of the thermistor expressed as a

decimal fraction (percent/100), and T – T(0) is the temperature difference written as an exponent of the quantity (1 – C).

Using this equation, we can calculate the resistance at 100°C (the boiling point of water) of a thermistor having a resistance of 10,000 ohms at 25°C (room temperature) assuming a temperature coefficient of 5%. Plugging these values into the equation, we would have

$$R(100) = 10000 \times (1 - 0.05) \uparrow (100 - 25)$$

then

$$
\begin{aligned}
R(100) &= 10000 \times (0.95) \uparrow 75 \\
&= 10000 \times (0.02134) \\
&= 213 \text{ ohms}
\end{aligned}
$$

When a thermistor is used to measure the temperature then the resistance, R(T), will be known and we will want to solve the equation for the temperature, T. To do this, we must rewrite the equation to solve for T:

$$\frac{R(T)}{R(0)} = (1 - C) \uparrow (T - T(0))$$

and by taking logarithms of both sides and rearranging:

$$\log R(T) - \log R(0) = [T - T(0)] \times \log(1 - C)$$

or

$$T = T(0) + \frac{[\log R(T) - \log R(0)]}{[\log(1 - C)]}$$

Although this is a fairly involved equation, it is one that a computer can do with ease. As a check on the equation, if we plug our previous answer of 213 ohms into the equation for R(T) and solve using the same other conditions as before, we obtain T = 100.04° (to five digits).

This brings up a very crucial point about making measurements. It would appear that the equation made a mistake of 0.04° more than it should have. The real problem is that we rounded off the value of R(T) to 213 instead of carrying any digits to the right of the decimal point. Had we plugged in 213.4 ohms instead of 213 we would have obtained T = 100.003°. The important point to remember is that our calculated results can never be any more precise than the measured value we use in the calculations. For example, if our measurement could only be made to the nearest (whole) ohm, then the uncertainty of the temperature we calculate would always be limited by the uncertainty of the measured resistance. To illustrate this problem, if we calculate T when R is 214 and 212, we obtain temperatures of 99.9° and 100.1°, respectively. Thus we can conclude that around 100° we could never measure the temperature to better than a tenth of a degree with a 1-ohm uncertainty in the resistance. Actually when using thermistors, the uncertainty in temperature gets worse as the temperature increases. Near room temperature, the uncertainty for our example problem is 0.002°.

For temperatures up to 300°F (150°C), the thermistor is probably the best choice of electrical thermometer for energy monitoring applications. Since its nonlinearity presents no problem to a computer calculation and its cost is low (about $1.00) it is a good candidate. Probably its greatest drawback is availability. Typically, thermistors are available from industrial suppliers and are not generally carried on the hobbyist (industrial surplus) market. This usually means that a minimum purchase is required and makes purchasing more expensive to an individual wanting to make a small purchase. One further point about cost is worth noting. The inexpensive thermistors that can be bought are not calibrated. This is a topic we will take up later. We observe here that calibrated thermistors are very expensive.

Analog-to-Digital Conversion

A basic fact of physical measurements is that almost all devices used to measure a physical property, such as temperature in our case, generate an *analog signal*. An analog signal can be represented as a voltage on a single wire that can assume *any value* within its operating range. A microcomputer can only accept a *digital signal* represented by eight wires each of which can assume only *one of two values* of the voltage. It is obvious that some means must be found to convert the analog signal into a digital signal before the computer can process the signal data. The usual solution is to use a linear integrated circuit called an analog-to-digital converter (ADC). Typically, the analog data can be converted into a 6-, 8-, 10-, or 12-bit digital value in 50 microseconds or less. Of course, the greater the resolution of the signal (larger the number of bits) and the faster the speed of conversion, the greater the cost of the ADC. If one is interested in converting many different analog signals, then either one ADC per signal is required or additional circuitry involving computer-controlled analog switches is necessary.

There are other less costly (and generally slower) techniques to accomplish the analog to digital conversion. There are two methods that input only one bit of information that the computer converts to an 8-bit (or more) count. These methods might be considered "software ADCs" since the computer is programmed to perform the analog to digital conversion. One of these methods uses a linear integrated circuit known as a voltage comparator in conjunction with a digital-to-analog converter (DAC) integrated circuit. Because a DAC is not as expensive as an ADC, this method enjoys considerable popularity. As noted previously, it has the disadvantage of taking a longer time to make a conversion: on the order of a few hundred microseconds. In this method, the two inputs to the comparator are supplied, respectively, by the analog signal to be measured and the analog output of the DAC. The computer, using one of a few standard algorithms, outputs a digital value to the DAC and inputs the one-bit output of the comparator. Depending on the logic state of this one-bit input, the computer searches for a digital value that equals the unknown analog signal.

A second method, which is the technique employed in the Energy Monitor Interface, uses a one-bit digital signal to convert an analog signal to a digital count. In this technique, the time that the digital signal is in its active logic state, say logic 1, is proportional to the value of the analog signal. In this type of software conversion, the computer program stays in a loop routine that inputs the one-bit signal and increments a counter register as long as the signal is a logic 1. This method is cheaper to implement than either the ADC or the DAC method. As in the previous case, its disadvantage is the long time required for conversion. Note that the method functions as a frequency counter with the upper frequency limit (shortest time count) determined by the execution time of one loop in the counting routine of the computer. Typical conversion time for 8-bit resolution is about 5 milliseconds. As we shall see, this method has the advantage of being able to measure eight analog signals simultaneously! It is applicable to analog signals that vary relatively slowly with time (tenths of a second per unit change) and originate from a variable resistance transducer. These are exactly the requirements demanded by our interest to measure eight different temperatures using thermistors.

This method uses an integrated circuit timer that produces a 5-volt (logic 1) pulse for a time period dependent on the value of the product of the resistance and capacitance (RC value) in a resistor-capacitor network wired to the timer. The IC timer is the 555 multivibrator wired in a monostable configuration. The circuit is shown in Fig. 2-1. In its quiescent or inactive state, the output of the 555 is at ground potential (logic 0). In this state, the current from the +5-V source through resistor R is led to ground internally through the 555 discharge (DSC) input at pin 7, and capacitor C remains discharged. The 555 is activated by a short active low pulse (logic 0) on its trigger input (TRG at pin 2). When the trigger pulse is received, the internal link to ground is opened and the capacitor starts to charge. Simultaneously the output at pin 2 goes to +5 V (logic 1). As charge accumulates on capacitor C, the voltage, V_c, across the capacitor (relative to ground) continues to rise. When V_c equals two-thirds of the supply voltage, the threshold input (THR at pin 6) reactivates the internal ground link which instantaneously discharges the capacitor and simultaneously returns the output to a logic 0. The duration of the output pulse, t, is directly proportional to the values of R and C.

Since we can substitute a thermistor for the resistor and use a fixed value capacitor in the circuit, then the duration of t is directly determined by the temperature of the thermistor. We have already established the relationship of the temperature, T, to the resistance, R, for the thermistor. It remains only to determine the relationship to R to the pulse width, t, to obtain the relationship of T to t.

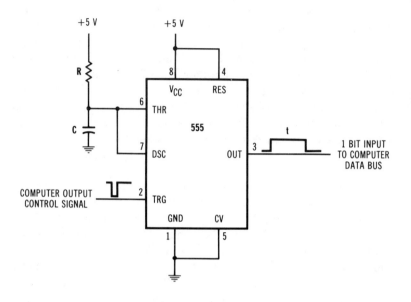

Figure 2-1
Monostable circuit.

The equation we start with is the basic charging time of an RC network:

$$V_c = V \times \left[1 - \exp \left(\frac{-t}{RC} \right) \right]$$

where V_c is the voltage across the capacitor (C in farads) at some time (t in seconds) after a charging current started through the resistor (R in ohms) from the voltage source (V in volts). Here $(-t/RC)$ is the exponent of the constant e, the base of natural logarithms, equal to 2.71828: that is 2.71828 is raised to the $(-t/RC)$ power. We specifically want to calculate the time it takes for V_c to build up to be equal to 2/3 of V: $V_c = 2 V/3$. Substituting and simplifying, we obtain:

$$\frac{2V}{3} = V \times \left[1 - \exp \left(\frac{-t}{RC} \right) \right]$$

dividing both sides by V:

$$\frac{2}{3} = 1 - \exp\left(\frac{-t}{RC}\right)$$

subtracting 1 from both sides:

$$\frac{-1}{3} = -\exp\left(\frac{-t}{RC}\right)$$

finally, taking the natural logs:

$$t = RC \ln 3$$

Since ln 3 is a constant equal to 1.0986, we find that (to three digits),

$$t = 1.10 \ RC$$

A sample calculation of t in seconds for a thermistor having 10,000 ohms resistance at room temperature and using a 1.0 μF capacitor yields:

$$t = (1.10)(10000)(0.000001)$$
$$= 0.011 \text{ second}$$
$$= 11 \text{ milliseconds}$$

This is a comparatively long time by computer standards. Anticipating what we shall determine later, a computer that operates at approximately 2 MHz (1.77 MHz for the TRS-80) could count to 573 in this time using the machine language subroutine listed in Listing 2-1.

```
        OUT (1),A      ;TRIGGER 555 TIMER
        LD C,0FFH      ;SET BIT MASK (MULTI-BIT COUNT)
COUNT,  INC DE         ;INCREMENT COUNTER
        IN (1),A       ;READ MONOSTABLE LEVEL
        XOR C          ;IS IT HIGH?
        JP Z, COUNT    ;YES: KEEP COUNTING
        .              ;NO: QUIT COUNTING
        .
        .
```

Listing 2-1. Assembly language counting routine

Semiconductor Thermometers

In Table 2-1, the semiconductor junction was also listed as an electrical thermometer. There are many references in the technical literature to diodes and transistors working as thermometers. The distinct advantage of using small signal diodes is that they are readily available and very inexpensive. The disadvantage is the complicated math involved in obtaining an explicit relationship between T and t when used in the 555 circuit just described. We shall briefly outline these problems so that they can be understood and appreciated. Our final solution will be to resort to an empirical expression in order to overcome the math obstacles.

Instead of using a thermistor, the Energy Monitor Interface uses a thermometer element consisting of four small signal diodes connected in series. Each quad diode thermometer (QDT) was wired in series with a fixed 10K resistor and a 1.0 μF tantalum

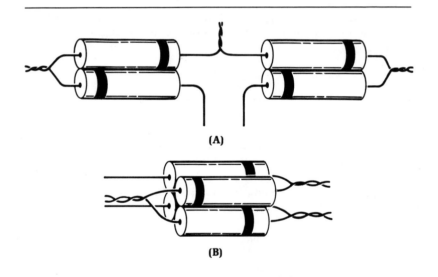

(A)

(B)

Figure 2-2
Quad diode thermometers.

capacitor between the + 5-V supply and ground in the RC network of a 555 timer. Each QDT is made from four 1N914 diodes having their leads twisted and soldered together as shown in Fig. 2-2. Insulated leads of 26-gage stranded wire were soldered to the two leads of the QDT. The insulated pair of leads were up to 25 feet long and were twisted to minimize inductive pick-up. After all leads were soldered, the body of the QDT was coated with epoxy resin (glue) and allowed to harden to form an insulated coating. Of the two configurations shown in Fig. 2-2, the open configuration (a) was used for the set-point thermometers and the folded configuration (b) was used for the outdoor thermometer. The open configuration is preferred for attachment to hot water pipes using plastic electrical tape because it allows each diode to be in contact with the pipe surface. The folded configuration is better as a noncontact (air) thermometer, since good thermal contact between all four diodes is maintained and temperature gradients are minimized.

The QDT-RC circuit shown in Fig. 2-3A shows the quantities involved in converting electrical current into a time pulse the duration of which is related to the temperature. We can analyze this circuit by examining certain special cases. First, consider the case where there are no diodes in the circuit, as illustrated in Fig. 2-3B. We know that the maximum current possible will be at the moment the switch is closed and the voltage drop across the capacitor is zero and across the resistor is V. As the current flows the voltage builds across the capacitor until the voltage drop across the resistor is zero. Therefore, the maximum current through the actual circuit (Fig. 2-3A) will be $I(0) = V/R$.

Furthermore, we know that at any moment the current, $I(t)$, will be proportional to the voltage drop across the resistor. Since the voltage drop across R is equal to the supply voltage, V, less the voltage that has built up on the capacitor, we have (by Ohm's law):

$$I = \frac{(V - V_c)}{R}$$

Now let us consider the second case, illustrated in Fig. 2-3C, in which the current limiting resistor is in series with four identical diodes. Ordinarily one uses the rule that the voltage drop across the silicon junction of a diode is 0.6 V. This is because of the characteristic current-voltage (I-V) curve of a diode. The I-V curve

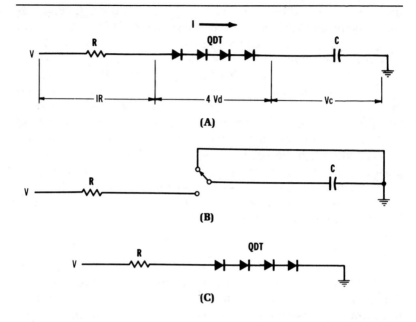

Figure 2-3
RC-QDT network.

is actually exponential as shown in Fig. 2-4, and the value of 0.6 volt corresponds to the voltage at which the current increases dramatically with each subsequent small increase in voltage at ordinary temperatures. Fig. 2-4 illustrates several aspects we want to consider. The I-V curves for four QDTs were experimentally determined at three different temperatures with four different current limiting resistors. The voltage drop V_d across each diode was obtained by dividing the voltage drop across all four diodes in the QDT by 4. The supply voltage for these curves was +5 V.

The straight lines passing through all six curves correspond to the limiting current equations derived above for the four resistance values listed. Because we have defined V_d as one-fourth of the voltage drop across a QDT and are using a voltage source of +5 V, the four straight lines all converge at a point on the V_d axis of $5/4 = 1.25$ volts when the current is zero. Although the figure does not extend below 0.3 volt, the values of the current when V_d is zero are given by Ohm's law: $I = 5/R$.

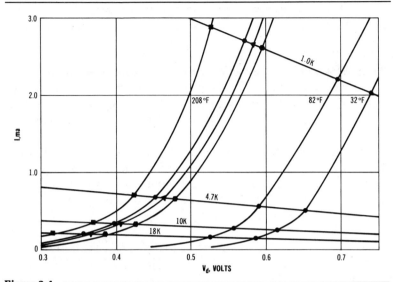

Figure 2-4
Characteristic diode curves.

At the same temperature (208°F in the figure), each of the four QDTs has its own unique curve. This means that each QDT will give a different response time in the 555 circuit and will have to be calibrated or in some way standardized against temperature. Now consider the three curves corresponding to the same QDT at three different temperatures (plotted with circular points in the figure). As the temperature decreases, the characteristic I-V curve shifts to the right corresponding to larger V_d values for a given current.

Finally, all six curves will intersect at the origin of the graph where both I and V_d are zero. The general mathematical equation for these curves is:

$$I = A \exp\left(\frac{B V_d}{T}\right)$$

where A and B are constants and differ for each QDT. In principle, these "constants" do not depend on the temperature. In fact, A and B are functions of T. It is this temperature dependence that makes the relationship between the time duration of the

37

monostable pulse and the temperature solvable only by experimentally determining the correct mathematical form of this equation.

We can, however, carry our analysis one step further by considering the effect of adding the capacitor and timer to the resistor-QDT circuit. The first effect of having the capacitor in the circuit will be to further limit the current due to the back-voltage which gradually builds on C. This back-voltage has the same effect as if the source voltage were reduced. Thus, in Fig. 2-5A, the I-V plot of one QDT shows a set of parallel limiting current lines corresponding to the increasing voltage on the capacitor, V_c. These lines all correspond to a source voltage of +5 V and a 1000-ohm current-limiting resistor.

There is an additional relationship that we can examine which exists between the voltage drop across the QDT and the voltage that builds up on the capacitor (relative to ground). Since the sum of the voltage drops across R, QDT, and C must equal the supply voltage, we have:

$$V = IR + V_c + 4V_d$$

Since I in this equation is an exponential function of V_d, it is apparent that the algebra is getting more and more complicated. We can solve this problem graphically instead of algebraically by using Fig. 2-5A to construct the plot of V_c versus V_d shown in Fig. 2-5B. The significant point to notice is that we can now begin to see how time becomes a measurable quantity related to the temperature. At the moment the 555 timer breaks the ground link, the current will be I(0), V_c will be zero, and V_d will be 0.7 V for the example QDT (read from Fig. 2-5A). Sets of values of V_c and V_d, which give the same value of I, can be constructed from the above equation and plotted as the sets of triangular legs shown in Fig. 2-5B. Finally, by connecting the vertices (corners) of the legs we obtain the "path" of I as V_c and V_d change for this particular QDT. Recall that the 555 timer will discharge the capacitor when $V_c = 2 V/3$ or 3.33 volts for a +5-V supply. The current at this instant is labeled I(t) in the figure.

We are now ready to deal with the final phase of the circuit

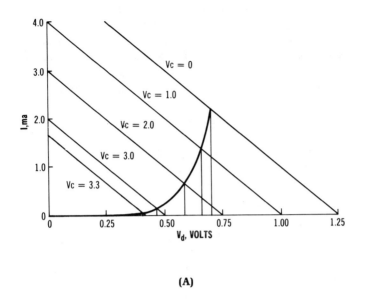

(A)

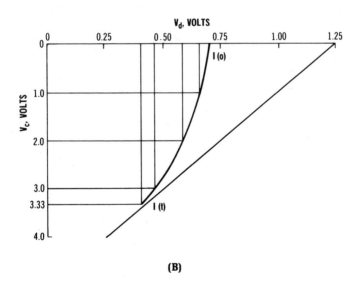

(B)

Figure 2-5
Limiting diode current to capacitor voltage.

analysis. We have seen so far that the current passing through the circuit starts at a value of I(0) and decreases continuously to a value of I(t) when V_c = 2 V/3. This current decreases according to an exponential function that depends on the temperature of the diodes. The 555 discharges at 2 V/3. For a given size of capacitor, it takes a specific amount of charge to reach 2 V/3. Since we know that the current indicates the rate of charging (coulombs/second), then the time duration of the monostable pulse equals the time it takes to move along the inclined path starting at point 0 and running to point t in the figure. Now, the greater the current, the shorter the time. We saw in Fig. 2-4 that the higher the temperature, the greater the current. Therefore, the higher the temperature, the shorter the time.

Summary

The following conclusions can be drawn from the discussion presented in this chapter:
1. The measurement of temperature can be made by a micro-computer which converts the output of an RC driven mono-stable into a count proportional to the pulse duration and consequently proportional to the temperature.
2. Eight individual temperatures can be measured simul-taneously using a single 8-bit I/O port.
3. Economical temperature sensors can be made from four small signal diodes connected in series in the RC network of the monostable timer circuit.
4. The temperature dependence of either the quad diode thermometer (QDT) or thermistor is a complicated algebraic expression which must be determined empirically by calibration.

Interface
Hardware

Chapter 3——————————————————————————

The interface circuit can be divided into three separate parts: the bus buffer and driver, the real-time clock, and the thermometer port. The interface is constructed on a standard wire-wrap board measuring 4 1/2 × 6 1/2 inches that has 44 contacts on a two-sided edge connector. The board layout indicating the positions of integrated circuits and other components is shown in Fig. 3-1. The connection between the interface board and the microcomputer bus lines is made with a 40-conductor flexible cable. The cable is terminated on the interface board with a double row 20-pin "socket header" located on the lower right edge of the board. The eight pairs of wires connected to the temperature sensors are terminated on the interface board with a 16-pin single-row socket header located above the bus cable header. A two-pin header is located in the upper left corner of the board to provide a 60-Hz ac signal of 16 rms volts for the clock circuit.

Power for the interface must be supplied from a separate power supply. Since the clock circuit will also require a − 12-V supply and because future interfacing projects will more than likely also require a + 12-V supply, it is strongly recommended that a power supply capable of providing + 5 V at 1.5 amps and + 12 V and − 12 V at 0.5 amp each be purchased. There are several sources for power supplies of this size available to hobbyists for about $30.00 which are frequently listed in the advertisements in the popular radio-electronics and microcomputing magazines. One important requirement when using more than one power supply

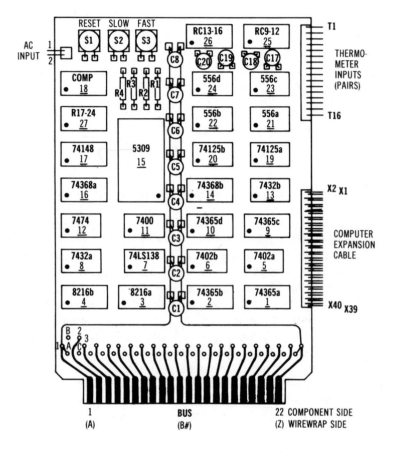

Figure 3-1
Component layout.

is that the electrical grounds from all supplies, including the one for the microcomputer be connected in common.

The power supply leads are connected directly to the edge connector contacts. Pads 1 and A (left end, both sides) are assigned to ground and pads 22 and Z (right end) are assigned to +5 V. Two pad assignments for the +5-V and ground power leads are made in order to allow for enhanced current conduction.

The power is distributed on the board by soldering 24 gage wire leads to the top ends of eight pairs of wire-wrap posts located along the center line of the board. Decoupling capacitors are also soldered across each pair of posts. Wire-wrap connections are made on the underside of each post to the + 5-V and ground pins of each IC socket. Pin 1 of each socket is indicated by a dot as shown in Fig. 3-1.

We shall use the signal names, pin numbers, and logic levels consistent with the TRS-80 Model I bus. Other microcomputer buses of 80-family microprocessors will most likely have all these signals available for interfacing although the names and the active logic states may differ. Except for the external power supply, the board edge connections are not used in this interface but allow for future expansion of the system. By wiring two or more edge connector sockets in parallel, additional boards can be connected through the buffered interface to the microcomputer. Although the assignment of the 44 pads on the interface bus is arbitrary, some planning in anticipation of future use is warranted. Since there has been no established industry standard for the 44-pin edge connector as a microcomputer bus, a few considerations are important. Foremost is making the bus assignment as practical as possible. In a series of articles published in American Laboratory magazine, the author proposed a microcomputer interfaced data acquisition system (MIDAS) bus based on the 44-pin edge connector. By assigning all signals required for data acquisition and control using accumulator I/O to the 22 pins on the back edge (pads A-Z), use of single-sided printed circuit boards is possible at a significant savings in future costs. These signals include the low address bus (A7-A0), the data bus (D7-D0), the I/O controls (IN*, OUT*), and four power pins (+ 5 V, + 12 V, – 12 V, and Ground). It should be noted that the assignment of letters to the 22 pads on the back edge of the board do not use the four letters which might be confused with the numbers 0 or 1: namely the letters G, I, O, and Q. The remaining 22 letters are assigned from right to left in alphabetical order facing the back side, i.e., from left to right when viewed from the component side. The second consideration for pin assignment should be some degree of systematic order instead of for convenience of the first board designed as was the case for both the S100 and TRS-80 buses. Consistent with these considerations, the suggested assignment for the MIDAS bus is listed in Table 3-1. The blanks in the assignment can be used for additional control signals that are not available on the TRS-80 bus.

Table 3-1. Microcomputer Interfaced Data Acquisition System (MIDAS) Bus

Pad#	Signal	Pad#	Signal
1	GND	A	GND
2		B	− 12 V
3	MW*	C	OUT*
4	MR*	D	IN*
5		E	D0
6		F	D1
7	INTA*	H	D2
8	INT*	J	D3
9		K	D4
10		L	D5
11		M	D6
12		N	D7
13	A8	P	A0
14	A9	R	A1
15	A10	S	A2
16	A11	T	A3
17	A12	U	A4
18	A13	V	A5
19	A14	W	A6
20	A15	X	A7
21	SYSRES*	Y	+ 12 V
22	+ 5 V	Z	+ 5 V

Bus Buffer

This part of the interface circuit intercepts all lines from the microcomputer. Fig. 3-2 shows the address bus drivers for all 16 address lines and the six control lines used for memory, input/output, and interrupt control. The driver circuit consists of four 74365 hex bus drivers. Each 74365 contains six tristate buffers. All six buffers are enabled with two active low enable

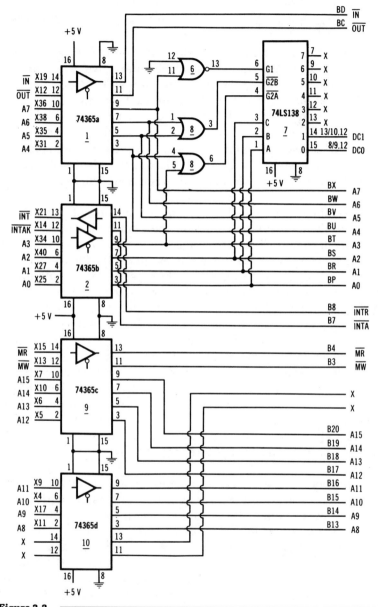

Figure 3-2
Address and control buffers and device decoder.

gates. For our purposes, the 16 address lines plus the six control lines are permanently enabled (active low) by grounding all eight enable control inputs. Since the interface circuit uses only 22 of the 24 drivers, 2 are left for future implementation by the user.

The 16 address lines labeled A15-A0 are output lines from the microcomputer. Of the six control lines, five are outputs: MR*(memory read), MW*(memory write), IN*(data input), OUT*(data output), and INTA*(interrupt acknowledge). The remaining control line is INT*(interrupt request) and is an input signal. Note that the conventions of using either an asterisk or placing a bar over the name of a signal are equivalent and indicate that the active state of the line is a logic zero (electrical ground) while the passive (or quiescent) state is a logic one (+ 5 V).

The remainder of the address and control circuit consists of running all these lines to pins on the board edge pads and of address decoding. The address decoding is made up of two sections. The first section includes the 74LS138 3-to-8 line decoder which is used to create eight separate I/O (input/output) device code pulses. The decoder chip has three input lines (labeled C, B, and A) and three enable control inputs (labeled G1, G2A*, and G2B*). Since the G1 enable is active high and the G2 enables are active low, it is necessary that all of them be in their appropriate active logic state before any of the decoder output lines will provide a unique signal. For future reference when we consider the clock circuit, it should be noted that the logic of the decoder output lines is active low (or logic zero) on only one of the eight outputs during the time that all three enable inputs are in their appropriate active states. Which output line goes low depends on the states of the three input lines.

By using combinatorial logic in the form of a pair of OR gates on a 7432 chip, the eight low address lines, A7-A0, can be reduced to the six inputs required for absolute decoding of the eight device codes on the 74LS138. Address lines A4 and A3 are ORed to drive enable G2A* and address lines A6 and A5 are ORed to drive G2B*. By inverting address line A7 with a spare 7402 2-input NOR gate having its second input permanently grounded, it can be seen that the decoder can only become activated when all five of these addresses are simultaneously at logic zero. Finally, by connecting the remaining three low address lines, A2-A0, to the decoder inputs the absolute values of the decoder outputs will correspond to the device codes 0 through 7. In particular, when all eight low address lines are at a logic zero, the output line "0" (at pin 15 of the 74LS138) will go to a logic zero. Of the 256 possible device codes ranging from 0 to 255, this decoder circuit will generate device codes 0 through 7 by making an active low pulse on each of the individual outputs of the 74LS138. Since the rest of the interface will use only device codes 0 and 1, the remainder of the device code output lines can be assigned to spare lines on the edge connector of the buffered bus for future use on other boards.

The second section of the address decoding circuit is concerned with controlling the direction of data flow on the bidirectional data bus. The circuit for this section is shown in Fig. 3-3. The data bus lines, D7-D0, are buffered with two 8216 4-bit parallel bidirectional bus drivers. Each chip consists of eight three-state buffers organized into two sets of four. The logic-equivalent circuit and truth table for the enable gates are shown in Fig. 3-4A. By permanently grounding the chip select enable (CS*), data being output on the microcomputer bus will appear on the interface bus as long as the data input enable (DE*) is at a logic one. In order to "turn the bus around" so that data can be input to the microcomputer from the interface, the DE* pin is brought to a logic zero with the set of NAND and NOR gates shown in Fig. 3-3. The simplified set of truth tables for this circuitry is presented in Fig. 3-4B. There are two sets of conditions that will turn the bus around. Either a data input for any device code below 128 or a memory read for any memory address above 32768 are the only conditions which will allow data to be input through the interface. These conditions are designed to be compatible with the TRS-80 Model I computer equipped with 16K of read/write memory. By limiting I/O devices to codes below 128, conflicts with the TRS cassette recorder (device code 255) are prevented. Similarly, memory addresses will not conflict on 16K machines. Although it would be possible to revise the logic to work above the 48K level for Model I 32K computers by connecting pin 5 of IC9 to pin 7 of IC9 (line A14), there are further complications with the 25 ms "heartbeat" of the Model I Expansion Interface.

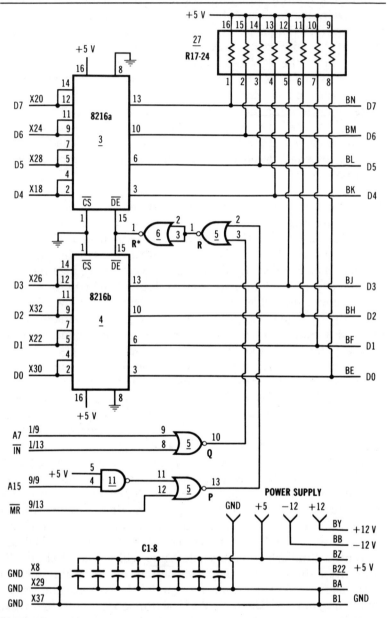

Figure 3-3
Bidirectional data bus buffer and power supply connections.

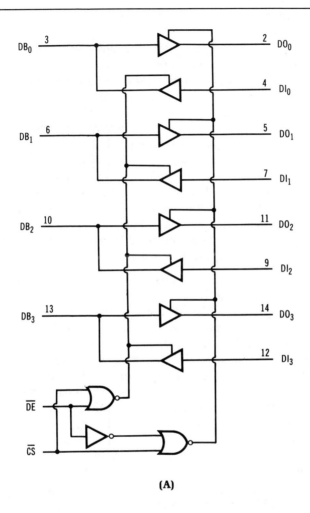

(A)

A15	MR*	A15*	P
1	0	0	1
0	0	1	0
1	1	0	0
0	1	1	0

IN*	A7	Q
0	0	1
0	1	0
1	0	0
1	1	0

P	Q	R	R* = DE*
0	0	1	0
0	1	0	1
1	0	0	1
1	1	0	1

(B)

Figure 3-4
8216 Logic equivalent circuit and truth tables.

Real-Time Clock

The reason the Model I Expansion Interface cannot be used with the Energy Monitor interface is that it contains an internal clock timer which is interrupt driven once every 25 ms. The internal clock is used in conjunction with the disk drive system and also to operate a software time-of-day clock. The disadvantage of the software clock is that when it is disabled and later reenabled, it has lost count of the intervening time. This is clearly unsatisfactory for our purposes. What is required is a clock that stores the real time which the computer can input on demand. The Energy Monitor interface clock interrupts the microcomputer once a second and forces the computer into a machine language routine which reads the six time digits and then returns to its previous function. The time required to perform the interrupt routine is 420 μs or about 0.04% of the total time.

Of the many clock chips available, the MM5309 (National) was chosen because it is readily available on the hobbyist market, it is inexpensive, and it provides all the functions that were deemed necessary for the energy monitor. It is a 28-pin DIP MOS integrated circuit which can operate between $+5$ V and -12 V. The chip operates in a multiplexed mode by using four pins to output the binary coded decimal value of one of the six digits (two each for hours, minutes, and seconds) and six pins to indicate by a logic zero which digit is currently being output. These six so-called "digit enable outputs" are labeled H10, H1, M10, M1, S10, and S1. In addition to the two power pins, there are nine control input pins. The remaining seven pins (labeled a-g) provide the code for displaying the digits on a set of seven-segment displays. These pins are not utilized in the energy monitor interface. The schematic of the clock circuit is shown in Fig. 3-5.

Of the nine control input pins on the 5309 clock chip, three are used to select operating mode. These are a choice between 12- or 24-hour display, 4- or 6-digit display, and 50- or 60-hertz frequency. To choose the first of each option, the respective pin must be connected to -12 V; to choose the second option, the pin is left unconnected and floats to $+5$ V through an internal pull-up resistor. The nine control lines are shown in the upper left-hand side of the 5309 block diagram. The MUX and AC inputs require additional passive components that are mounted on a 16-pin DIP

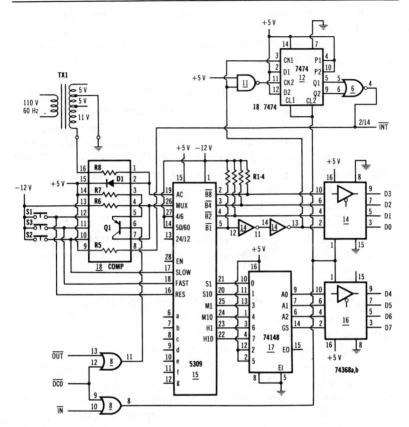

Figure 3-5
Clock port.

header labeled IC18. The AC input is the 60-hertz timing signal used by the clock chip for its fundamental counting frequency. Internal circuitry on the clock chip can accept a sine wave signal at this pin and shape it appropriately. The signal must swing between the operating voltages of this chip, which in our case is $+5$ V (V_{dd}) and -12 V (V_{ss}). We have chosen to obtain this signal from the 16-V secondary of a small transformer operating directly off a 110-V primary. This gives a stability for the signal frequency as dependable as the power line. The particular transformer used is a digital clock transformer (Radio Shack No. 273-1520) having a 5 V–5 V–11 V series of taps on its secondary winding. By grounding the first 5-V tap, a 25-V peak-to-peak signal is obtained at the other lead and swings between +12 V and –12 V. The signal is fed through a 100K resistor to limit its current and clamped with a small diode to the +5 V dc supply so that the input requirements of the ac pin are satisfied.

In the same manner as the other control lines, the MUX control operates between +5 V and –12 V. Each transition from +5 V to –12 V advances the selection of the time digit in the cyclic order: S1–S10–M1–M10–H1–H10. The transition is made by connecting the base of a 2N3905 pnp transistor to the TTL level Device Select Pulse (OUT 0*) output of an OR gate. During its quiescent time, the OR gate is at a logic one which leaves the base of the transistor on and the MUX pin floats to +5 V. When a device select pulse is generated by the computer, the base is turned off and the MUX pin is pulled to –12 V. Thus each OUT 0 command from the computer advances the time digit being output on the BCD lines of the clock.

The four remaining control pins are used respectively to reset the clock to zero, advance the hours digits (Fast), advance the minutes digits (Slow), and disable the bcd outputs. The first three lines are taken to the spare pins on the component socket. A jumper wire from the –12-V pin to any of the three pins can be used to manually implement these controls. Alternatively, the reset and advance pins can be connected to momentary switches as shown in the schematic. The hours and minutes advance controls operate at a one-per-second rate as long as the pin is held at –12 V. Because the disable control is not of any value to the energy monitor it was not wired to a momentary switch. The momentary switches are located in the upper left corner of the interface board (see Fig. 3-1).

We now examine the clock output lines and how they are interfaced to the microcomputer. The six-digit enable lines (S1, etc.) are connected to the inputs of a 74148 Priority Octal Encoder. The 74148 has four output lines that provide the binary coded decimal value of the highest (hence priority) input channel which is at a logic zero. We actually need not be concerned with the priority of the encoding since the digit enable lines of the clock chip never output more than one logic zero at a time. By permanently tying input channels 2 and 5 to a logic one (+5 V) we can force the bcd "address" values to provide a space between the hours and minutes digits and between the minutes and seconds digits. The encoded digit address is connected to lines D7-D4 of the data bus through a set of tristate inverters. In both cases of the digit address and the digit value, the inputs to the tristate buffers from the clock chip are complemented and must be inverted for the computer to read the proper value. For the bcd digit values to be TTL compatible, the lines (B4*-B1*) must be pulled down to – 12 V through the set of 1/2 watt 7.5K resistors. These outputs are capable of driving only one standard TTL load, however. Because we shall need to drive more than one load from the B1* pin, a pair of spare tristate inverters are permanently enabled and used to increase the fan out of the B1* line.

As we shall see later when we consider the program for operating the clock with the computer, we can ensure that the S1 line remains active when the computer is not interacting with the clock. When this is true, the digit value outputs of the clock chip (B4*-B1*) will continually count from zero through nine at a one per second rate. Since the least significant bit, B1*, of the bcd output changes its logic state with each successive count, we can use this change of state to drive a once-per-second interrupt generator. The circuit has a 7474 Dual Data Latch with its two independent clock inputs connected to the inverted and re-inverted (via the NAND gate) signals from B1*. Since the 7474 latches on the positive edge, or 0-to-1 transition, of its clock signal, both positive and negative edges of B1* alternately drive the Q outputs of the latches to a logic one. By NORing these outputs, a train of one-per-second pulses will be produced provided the latches are cleared (reset to logic zero) within the 1 second interval before the next edge drives the other latch. When any INT* pulse is detected by the computer, an interrupt service routine is executed which inputs the two bcd values of the clock (address and value of a time digit) onto the data bus and simultaneously clears the 7474 latches. A timing diagram of this sequence of events is shown in Fig. 3-6.

Thermometer Port

In Chapter 2 we discussed the use of the 555 Timer wired in the

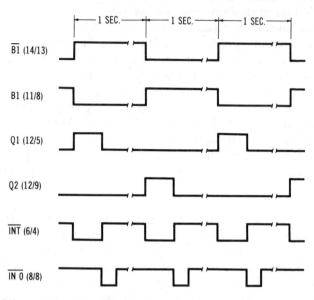

Figure 3-6
Timing diagram for the 1-Hz interrupt.

monostable configuration as a means of converting an analog signal into a 1-bit (digital) signal having a pulse time duration proportional to the magnitude of the analog signal. The schematic for the eight independent thermometers possible with one data byte is shown in Fig. 3-7. In place of the 555 integrated circuit, the 556 Dual Timer is used. It is a 14-pin DIP containing two independent 555-type timers sharing common power-supply pins. Since the Quad Diode Thermometer (QDT) was used in this system, each is shown connected in series with the resistor between +5 V and the Threshold and Discharge inputs of each timer. The 10K resistor and the 0.1 μF tantalum capacitor for each thermometer are mounted on 16-pin DIP headers with four QDTs per DIP socket. The leads for the QDTs are twisted wire pairs and were up to 25 feet long. Each pair of timers on all four 556 ICs are wired identically.

Each timer output is connected through a tristate buffer to one of the lines of the data bus. The tristate buffers are 74125s having their individual enable pins connected in parallel to the Device

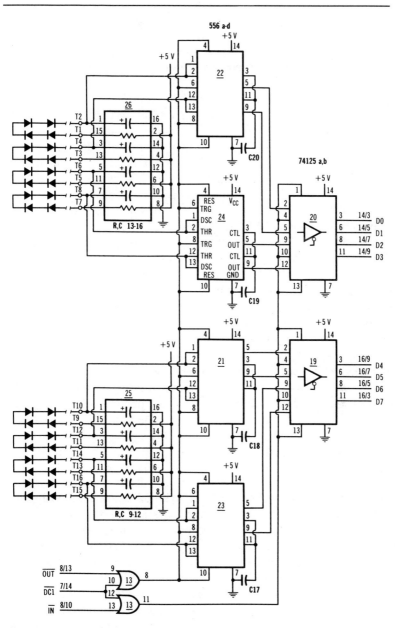

Figure 3-7
Thermometer port.

Select Pulse IN 1*. The Device Select Pulse OUT 1* is connected to both the Reset pin and the Trigger pin of each timer. By simultaneously resetting the timer each time it is triggered, a complete recharge of the newly discharged capacitor is assured. In this way false times are prevented if for some reason a second OUT 1 command were executed before all eight timers had timed out from an earlier command. At first glance it may seem odd that 16 inputs (8 Triggers plus 8 Resets) are being driven by one TTL output having a drive capability of 16 mA. If the 556 were a TTL IC this would clearly be an overload of the normal fan out of 10 for the 7432 OR gate that is driving these inputs. However, the current requirements of the Reset and Trigger inputs are 0.1 mA and 2 μA respectively, and all eight pairs of inputs represent a total load of only a little more than one half of a normal TTL load. The two Bypass pins of each 556 IC are connected in parallel to an isolation capacitor. These four capacitors are mounted below the two RC DIP header sockets as shown in Fig. 3-1.

If thermistors are used instead of QDTs, the fixed resistors in the timer RC circuit would be replaced with jumper wires on the DIP headers. The only type of thermistor that has been tested with the thermometer port is a 20K (at 25°C) small bead type. Neither self-heating of the thermistor nor the effect of lead length on the thermistor temperature characteristics was evaluated. In the case of the QDT used as the outdoor thermometer, the lead length was included in the calibration.

Construction Details

The parts for the three circuits of the interface are listed in Appendix A. This system was constructed using wire-wrapping techniques with the various components placed as shown in Fig. 3-1. The positions of the components shown in this figure are approximate since it is not precisely to scale. Therefore, the first step should be to determine the specific locations of all sockets and wire-wrap posts so that sufficient space is available where it is needed. Once this has been done, the sockets may be cemented in place, taking care to position the pin 1 corner of each correctly. Bathtub caulking compound (silicone) serves as a very adequate cement for the sockets. Care must be exercised when applying any cement (or glue, if used) not to insulate the socket pins with a covering of the adhesive. The three cable headers were carefully epoxied in position to provide the extra strength necessary for their use. The individual wire-wrap posts (shown as small squares in Fig. 3-1) were positioned and pressed into place. These posts were also used for the 44-pin edge connectors (not illustrated in the figure) and were soldered to the pads on the appropriate side of the board. The various components connected to the wire-wrap posts were also soldered to the tops of the posts. Solid wire (26 gage) was used for the + 5-V and Ground leads with lengths of insulation left between the wire-wrap posts.

Once all the preliminary steps are completed the wire wrapping can be undertaken. It is best to wire *all* power and ground connections first. Sockets in the same row on the board can be chained in series to the power supply post in that row. Be particularly careful to include the power leads to the various gates and buffer chips since these are not explicitly shown in the circuit schematics. All leads should be neatly routed on the board and kept short enough that they lie against the board. Care should be taken to avoid a "rat's nest" appearance.

It is a good idea to use a transparent colored felt tip pen to trace each pin to pin connection on the schematic as soon as it is made on the board. By completing the wiring for each of the four schematics (Figs. 3-2, 3-3, 3-5, and 3-7) before proceding to the next, the chance of missing a connection will be significantly decreased.

Summary

This completes our discussion of the design and construction details of the three sections of the Energy Monitor Interface. The special characteristics of each circuit are summarized in the fol- lowing list:

A. *INTERFACE*
  1. All address, data, and control lines from the microcomputer are buffered and brought out to a 44-pin edge connector.

2. The 16-bit address bus is permanently enabled.
3. The buffered data bus is enabled for output except when IN commands for device codes less than 128 or when memory read commands for addresses above 32K are executed by the microcomputer: at these times the data bus is enabled for input.
4. Device codes 0 through 7 are decoded from the low address bus with device codes 0 and 1 dedicated to the Clock and Thermometer ports, respectively (both for input and output). The remaining six device codes are not used.

B. CLOCK

1. The 24-hour, 6-digit time-of-day clock drives the computer interrupt request line at a one-per-second rate.
2. The clock time is manually set with three pushbutton switches mounted on the circuit board.
3. The base timing input to the clock is obtained from a clipped + 5-V to – 12-V, 60-hertz signal obtained from a small (30 mA) transformer.
4. Each of the six time digits must be separately input to the computer as two bcd digits (4 bits each) packed in one byte. The most significant bcd digit on data lines D7–D4 identifies the position of the time digit, that is its relative "address," and the least significant bcd digit provides the value of the time digit.

C. THERMOMETER PORT

1. Eight parallel "RC" time constant thermometers are accessible through one input/output port.
2. Each thermometer may be placed up to (at least) 25 feet from the interface board.
3. Management of the thermometers and evaluation of their temperatures is completely under software control of the computer.
4. Thermometer elements may be either thermistors or four series-connected small signal diodes.

Interface Software

Given the design characteristics of the Clock and Thermometer ports described in the preceding chapter we now need to consider the machine language programs required to service the ports. The complete assembler listing of these routines is given in Appendix B. The program plus the memory space used for data storage are located at the top of the 16K read/write memory. The program occupies 564 bytes with an additional 880 bytes used for data.

On power-up, Reset, and after every interrupt request, the microprocessor's interrupt request line is automatically disabled. The line remains disabled until it is specifically enabled by a machine instruction. On power-up and after a Reset, there will have to be a special initialization routine that will accomplish three tasks, the last of which will be to enable the interrupt. The other two tasks require further elaboration.

One of these tasks is to establish the mode in which the microprocessor will handle interrupts. We noted in Chapter 1 that there are three types of interrupt handling: single-line, vectored, and polled. For the Z80 microprocessor, which is used in the TRS-80 Models I and III and many S-100 systems, machine language commands are used to select the Mode of interrupt handling. The instruction mnemonics are IM0, IM1, and IM2, where IM is the abbreviation for Interrupt Mode. IM0 duplicates the vectored interrupt capabilities of the 8080 microprocessor. In this mode, the microprocessor "expects" the data bus to be holding a one byte instruction (vector) when it activates the INTA control output line. Typically, the one byte vector is one of the eight Restart instructions: mnemonic RST 'x'. These are the subroutine CALL commands which have implicit call addresses. The IM1 command of the Z80 places the microprocessor in a single-line interrupt mode where it does not "expect" a vector but assumes one specific address which is the same as the RST 7 command of the 8080. The hexadecimal address for the Mode 1 interrupt is 0038 (decimal 56).

Because the software is written specifically for the TRS-80 Model I, the initialization routine will include execution of the IM1 instruction. For systems other than the TRS-80, some modification of the hardware will have to be made in order to effect a single-line interrupt. For 8080 microprocessor systems, a vector will have to be "jammed" onto the data bus. By using the RST 7 command this is relatively easy since RST 7 has the code FF hex), that is, all eight bits are at logic one, and this is the code that would be read by a nonexistent (unconnected) port. An alternate technique is possible with 8080 systems that also use the 8228 Systems Controller integrated circuit. By pulling the INTA output of the 8228 (pin 23) to +12 V through a 1K pull-up resistor, the system will duplicate the Z80 Mode 1 interrupt control. For systems that use the 8085 microprocessor, one of the three single-line interrupts could be used: RST 5.5, RST 6.5, or RST 7.5.

There is one more feature of this task that must be considered. For the TRS-80 and all other systems which have read-only memory at high address 00 (hex), the subroutine call address for RST 7 must hold a three-byte Jump instruction to someplace in read/write memory. For the TRS-80, the location of the jump is to hex address 4012 (16402 decimal). There are three memory locations available starting at this address that are loaded by the BASIC monitor on power-up with the decimal codes: 251(=EI, enable interrupt), 201(=RET, return), 0(=NOP, no operation). The initialization routine must write over these three instructions with a second three-byte Jump instruction to the starting address of the interrupt service subroutine at the top of read/write memory.

The second task that needs to be included in the initialization routine concerns adjusting the clock output to the S1 digit to generate the once-a-second interrupt request described in Chapter

3. This part of the routine consists of outputting a Device Select Pulse to advance the clock multiplexer and then inputting the clock byte and evaluating the most significant 4 bits to determine whether it is the position address of the S1 digit. Each multiplexing pulse advances the clock output to the next digit in the order described previously. When the S1 digit is found, this portion of the routine is completed. A flowchart summarizing the initialization routine, labeled CLKEN (clock enable), is shown in Fig. 4-1 and presents the three tasks in order: (1) set clock to S1, (2) load second Jump command, (3) set interrupt mode and enable interrupt.

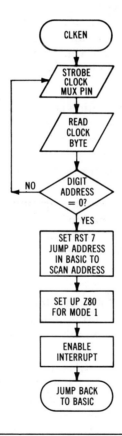

Figure 4-1
CLKEN flowchart.

Interrupt Service Routine

The initialization routine is executed using the "SYSTEM" command followed by the "/address" command on the TRS-80, where the address is the decimal value of the starting address of CLKEN. The second to last instruction in this routine before returning to the BASIC monitor is the EI command. The Enable Interrupt instruction does not take effect until the subsequent instruction has been executed. This guarantees that an interrupt can never occur while the computer is in its interrupt service routine. However, once the computer has returned to the BASIC monitor the Clock interface will start interrupting the microcomputer once every second. Because the CLKEN routine has written the address of the interrupt service subroutine into memory, then with each interrupt request the computer will execute a subroutine CALL to the service subroutine.

The first task of the service routine is to update the time of day by providing the current value of the six time digits for storage in computer memory. This, however, is only one of the tasks we wish to have performed. In addition, we want the temperatures at the thermometer port read periodically, an hourly record of the high and low outdoor temperature for the past 24 hours, an hourly record of the time-on for each of the remaining seven temperature sensors, and a monthly summary of these records. Therefore, the service routine must update its data collection as well as scan the time and temperature. The program is labeled SCAN and is flowcharted in Fig. 4-2.

As can be seen from the flowchart, there are four subroutines within the SCAN service routine: CLOCK, TEMP, DAY, and HOUR. The labels of these subroutines are self-explanatory. Note that, here again, the last step is to re-enable the interrupt before returning to the BASIC monitor. The first step in SCAN is to save the contents of all registers on the stack while the last step preceding the EI command is to restore all of these registers. In this way, except for the time lost for execution, the BASIC monitor will pick up right where it left off with the program that was being executed prior to the interrupt.

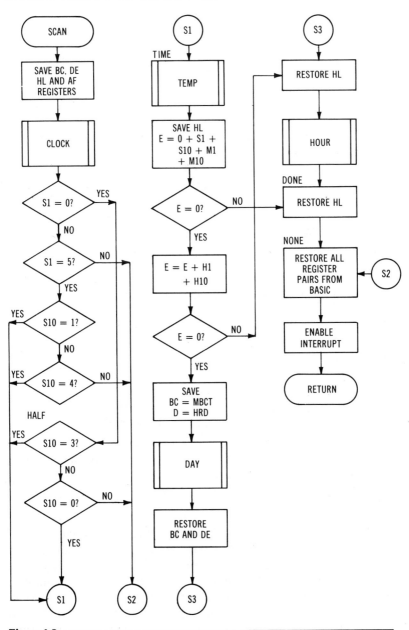

Figure 4-2
SCAN flowchart.

Clock Subroutine

The first subroutine executed in SCAN is CLOCK. This subroutine is flowcharted in Fig. 4-3. It is executed with each interrupt, that is, once each second. The object of this subroutine is to read all six digits of the time being kept by the clock chip and write the value of each digit into a memory register in the computer. The most convenient memory registers to use are those in the upper right corner of the video display. Since the data byte that is input from the clock consists of two bcd digits (position address and value), it must be unpacked after it is read. The video memory address of the upper right corner for the TRS-80 is hexadecimal 3C3F (decimal 15423). This should be the address of the S1 digit. Now the remaining digits have bcd position addresses that increase with S10 = 1, M1 = 3, M10 = 4, H1 = 6, and H10 = 7. If these values are, in turn, subtracted from the S1 memory address, they will give memory addresses appropriate for reading the time on the video screen in the normal left to right sequence. Note also that by skipping the relative positions of 2 and 5 in the encoding, there will be blank spaces provided between each pair of time digits (hours, minutes, and seconds).

Once the calculation of the memory address has been completed for a time digit, it remains to convert the bcd digit value into the ASCII code expected by the video decoder of the computer to form the numeral on the screen. Since we will only be displaying numerals, this is an easy conversion and amounts to adding a hexadecimal value of 30 to the bcd digit.

Recall that on entering the CLOCK subroutine at the start of SCAN the digit being output by the clock is the S1 digit. In order to be certain that the S1 digit is on the clock at the end of this subroutine and preserve the once-a-second interrupt generator, the digits are read by the computer in the order: S10, M1, M10, H1, H10, S1. Once the multiplexing has returned to the S1 digit and all six digits have been read, the subroutine is finished and a return to SCAN is executed.

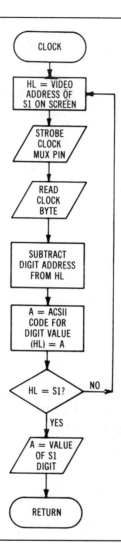

Figure 4-3
CLOCK flowchart.

Data Acquisition

As indicated in the SCAN flowchart (Fig. 4-2), the next sequence of steps is to decide if the current time is on the quarter-minute, i.e., at 0, 15, 30, or 45 seconds. If it is not, there are no additional operations required and a jump to the end of the routine is executed for a return to BASIC. If, on the other hand, the time is on a quarter-minute, there is further processing to be done. There are two reasons for picking 15-second intervals for data acquisition times. First, the typical response time of the thermometers is around 10 to 20 seconds so that shorter times would not provide any more meaningful measurements. Second, for the seven set-point measurements, if an hourly record for the current day is kept, there are 240 quarter-minutes per hour. Since one byte of data can store up to 256 counts, then a full count of 240 fits neatly within the capacity of one data byte per set-point thermometer per hour.

Memory Map

The remaining three subroutines in SCAN consist of the data acquisition (TEMP) and data processing (HOUR and DAY) routines. Before proceeding with a description of these routines, it will be worthwhile to review what kind of data and how much we plan to handle. Table 4-1 contains the series of five data tables stored between the end of the program and the top of memory. The table lists the decimal starting addresses of each of the data tables, the boundaries of the five data tables marked by the name of the table, and a byte ordered description of the (column) entries in each row. Each slash mark (/) indicates one data byte and the ellipsis (. . .) marks repeated bytes.

The data tables are labeled BUF, BASE, CTEMP, DAY and MONTH. Briefly, their respective functions are as follows. BUF is the table used for storing the current (15 second) thermometer reading. It is 24 bytes long consisting of eight sets of three bytes: one set for each of the eight thermometers. BASE is a table for storing the time-on count (in one byte) for each of the seven set-point thermometers in 15-second increments for each hour of the past 24 hours. In addition to the 24 memory locations necessary for each set-point thermometer, the value of the set point is stored in two bytes preceding the 24 hourly bytes. This table occupies 182 locations (26 × 7). The CTEMP table stores a two-byte value of the current outdoor temperature. Since each temperature value is stored as a time count and not as degrees, a two-byte value can range from 0 to a value of 65,535. Typical values for the Quad

Table 4-1. TNT Memory Map of Data Tables

First Decimal Address	TABLE NAME: Byte Format. Description of Table
31888	BUF: DC Mask/DC Lbyte/DC Mbyte. DC = Device Code Typical for 8 Devices with 3 bytes per device. 16-bit value of most recent Temperature Count. Ordered from shortest count to longest count. Memory locations = $3 \times 8 = 24$ bytes.
31912	BASE: SP(n)Lbyte/SP(n)Mbyte/Hour(0)count/ . . . /Hour(23)count. SP(n) = 16-bit Set-Point value of Device n. Hour Count = Count of 15 sec. Time-on intervals. Typical for 7 Devices with 26 bytes per device. Ordered from Device 7 to Device 1. Memory locations = $7 \times (2 + 24) = 182$.
32094	CTEMP: CT Lbyte/CT Mbyte CT = Current Temperature Count 16-bit value for Device 0. Memory locations = 2.
32096	DAY(CTEMP + 2): LT Lbyte/LT Mbyte/HT Lbyte/HT Mbyte. LT = Lowest Temperature Count for Device 0. HT = Highest Temperature Count for Device 0. 16-bit value of Count. Typical for 24 hours with 4 bytes per hour. Ordered from Hour 0 to Hour 23. Memory locations = $24 \times 4 = 96$.
32192	MONTH(MTOP-575): ST(7)Lbyte/ST(7)Mbyte/ . . . / ST(0)Mbyte/LT Lbyte/LT Mbyte/HT Lbyte/HT Mbyte. ST = Sum of Time-on Count per Device per Day. 16-bit value of Count. (LT and HT as defined above.) Typical for 32 day with 18 bytes per Day. Ordered from 1 Day Previous to 32 Days Previous. Memory locations = $32 \times (14 + 4) = 576$.
32767	(MTOP)

Diode Thermometers over the ambient range lie between 1000 and 10,000. Subsequent rows in the DAY table represent each hour in the 24- hour day. Each of these rows consists of the two-byte value of the highest temperature measured during the hour and the two-byte value of the lowest temperature measured during the hour. There are 98 locations used in this data table (2 + 24 × 4). The fifth data table, MONTH, stores a 32-day record with each row of the table saving a summary of daily data. For each row (day), there are seven two-byte entries holding the sum of quarter-minute intervals that each of the set-point thermometers were "on," plus the four bytes necessary to store the daily high and low outdoor temperature. This table occupies 18 × 32 or 576 locations.

Temperature Measurement

The temperature measurement subroutine, TEMP, resets and triggers all 555 timers and then measures the duration of the eight individual monostable pulses. The duration of the pulse for each thermometer is stored as a count of two bytes in the BUF table. The two-byte count is preceded by a one-byte code to identify the thermometer. After all eight counts have been obtained, each of the seven set-point thermometer counts is compared with its corresponding set-point value. If the count is numerically less than the set-point value, then the current temperature is greater and the time-on count for that thermometer is incremented in its appropriate hour data byte in the BASE table. After the seven set-point thermometers have been compared and their current hour time-on count taken care of, the outdoor thermometer temperature count is transferred from its location in BUF fo the two-byte location in the CTEMP table. The current temperature count is then compared to the current hour high and low temperature counts stored in DAY. If one or the other of these is exceeded by the current temperature, it is replaced by it in the table. The routine is then finished and the program returns to the SCAN routine.

The flowchart for TEMP is shown in Figs. 4-4A and 4-4B. The first half of the subroutine, shown in Fig. 4-4A, initializes the 16-bit BC register and the 8-bit D register of the microprocessor and saves these values on the stack. It then evaluates the temperature counts for all eight thermometers and stores their values in BUF. Finally it restores BC and D, and initializes the E register for the second half of the subroutine.

The BC register is used to point to the low order byte of the set-point value of thermometer No. 7. This address is the first location in the BASE data table. The program next evaluates the hour-of-day, i.e., from 0 (midnight) to 23 (11 P.M.), to serve as a displacement to be added to the BC address to determine the address where the time-on count for the current hour is stored. Note that an extra value of two must be added to allow for the two bytes occupied by the set-point value. On entering the subroutine, the HL register pair already points to the address of the H10 digit of the clock. Once the D register is loaded, it and BC are PUSHed onto the stack for later use. In the next step, the HL and DE registers are prepared for the temperature counting. HL points to the first address of the BUF data table. DE will serve as the 16 bit counter for the temperature counts and is started at a value of zero.

Recall that each thermometer uses a single line on the data bus. We can number the thermometers with the data line each uses: thermometer No. 7 on D7, etc. The program is written to use thermometers 1 through 7 as the set-point sensors and thermometer No. 0 (on D0) as the outdoor thermometer. Any other arrangement will require program revisions. The 555 timers are initialized with an output control pulse to device No. 1 as noted above. A mask byte stored in register C of all 1s is initialized and the DE counter incremented by one count. The monostable pulses will all be high on the first count since they were just triggered. The eight data lines are input from device No. 1 and the data byte compared to the mask. If the mask and the data byte agree, the program loops back to increment the DE counter. The program will stay in this loop until one or more of the thermometer monostables times-out and the output goes to logic zero. When this happens, the data line will be read as a zero and the mask will not agree with the data byte.

The program then branches (at point T2 in Fig. 4-4A), stores the data byte in BUF as the code for which thermometer(s) timed-out, and stores the two-byte value of the count for the thermometer(s)

69

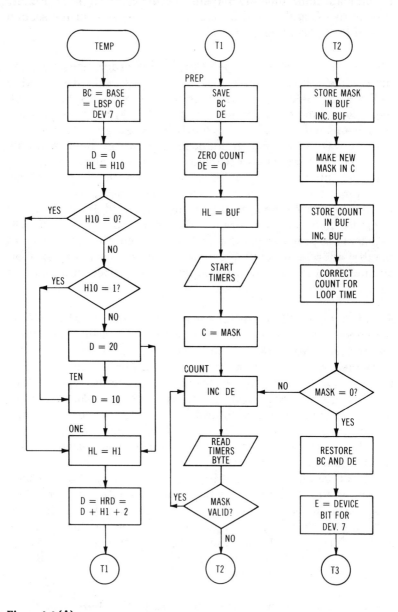

Figure 4-4 (A)
TEMP flowchart.

70

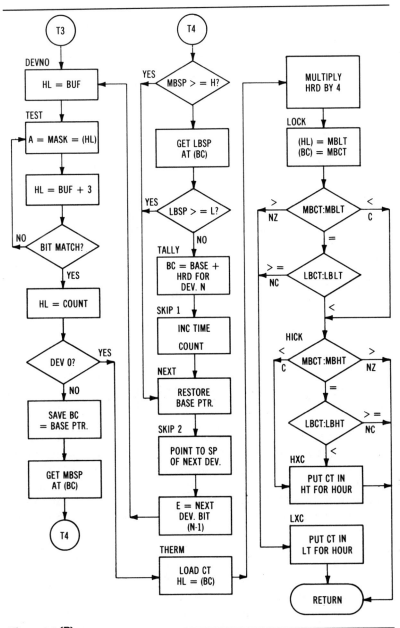

Figure 4-4 (B)
TEMP flowchart.

in the next two locations. In the process, a new mask is formed for the remaining thermometers. The count in DE is corrected for the time lost out of the counting loop and the new mask is checked to see if all bits are zero, indicating that all eight thermometers have timed-out. If the mask has any nonzero bits, the program jumps back to the counting loop. Otherwise, the program restores its initial pointers in registers BC and D and proceeds to its second half.

It should be noted that the thermometers are read in parallel with the BUF table filling in order of increasing count. Thus, the shortest count is stored in the first entry in BUF and the longest count is stored as the last entry. This is a much faster routine than reading the thermometers serially, i.e., one at a time. If they were read serially, the time delay for the interrupt routine on the quarter minute could take a few tenths of a second. Although this may not seem too long, it would result in dropping a character for a moderately fast typist entering text from the keyboard in a BASIC monitor background program.

Beginning at point T3 in the second half of the subroutine in Fig. 4-4B, the thermometer codes in BUF (every third entry) are searched consecutively starting with thermometer No. 7 and proceeding to thermometer No. 0. Register E is used to compare the bit number of the thermometer with the mask value stored in BUF. For thermometers 7 through 1, the high byte and, if necessary, the low byte of the count in BUF is compared to the set-point high and low bytes, respectively. If the BUF entry is smaller, the time-on count at the current hour entry in the BASE table is incremented. The BC pointer to the set-point value of the next thermometer is calculated, the bit number in E is set, and the operation is repeated. When the current count for thermometer No. 0 is retrieved from the BUF table, the program branches to the last section of the subroutine, labeled THERM.

In this part of the program, the count of the current outdoor temperature is stored in the first two bytes of the CTEMP table. Because there are four bytes stored per hour in the CTEMP table, the hour displacement value is multiplied by four by shifting the bits in register D two places to the left. The two-byte current-temperature count is consecutively checked (most significant byte first) against the current-hour low temperature count stored in CTEMP. At two places in the flowchart, a three branch decision box is shown to indicate the choice of greater than, equal to, and less than. This is actually two conditional jumps in the program which must be executed in the order given in the listing in order to work properly. If the low temperature comparison is successful and the current temperature count is greater (temperature is lower) than the value stored for the current hour, a replacement is made. When this is the case, the high temperature comparison is not made. If the low temperature comparison is unsuccessful, then the high temperature is compared to the current temperature. The subroutine is finished when these comparisons are completed and a return to the SCAN routine is made.

Data Management

The remaining two subroutines, HOUR and DAY, are file management routines. The HOUR subroutine is executed when the minutes and seconds digits of the clock are all zeros. However, when the hour digits are also zeros, the DAY subroutine must be executed before the HOUR subroutine. This sequence of decisions is made in the SCAN routine. The reason for this precedence of the DAY subroutine is to preserve the data stored in the midnight hour before it is reinitialized by the HOUR subroutine.

The DAY subroutine manages the 32-row MONTH table where each row of the table is a summary of nine two-byte daily entries. Seven entries are the total time-on counts in quarter minutes of the set-point thermometers. The eighth and ninth entries are the daily low and high outdoor temperature counts, respectively. As noted previously, the MONTH table is stored at the top of memory. The DAY subroutine advances each of the 32-day entries up one row by pushing the oldest entry out of the top and making room at the bottom for the day just completed at midnight. The process is shown in the loop labeled MORE in Fig. 4-5. It might be noted here that this type of block move can be written in fewer steps with the expanded instruction set of the Z80 microprocessor. It was written using only the 8080 subset to maintain compatibility with all microprocessors of the 80 family.

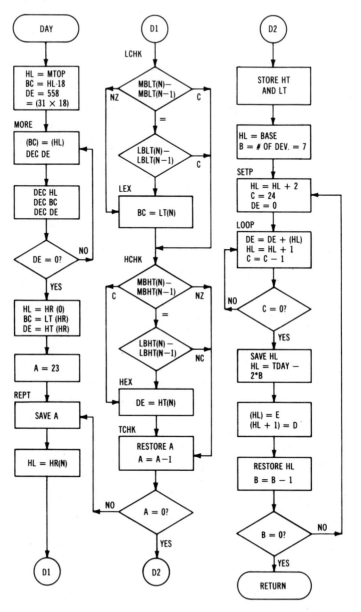

Figure 4-5
DAY flowchart.

The next portion of the program searches the 24 hourly entries for the lowest and highest temperature counts in the DAY table. The BC and DE 16-bit registers are used to hold the midnight hour values which are successively compared with the subsequent hourly entries. In each instance where a successive hourly entry is lower in temperature (higher in count) than the value stored in BC, it replaces that value; similarly, for the high temperature value in DE. The HL register holds the address of the count being compared. The two branching networks, LCHK and HCHK, perform the comparison and exchange steps. After all 24-hour values have been examined, the subroutine branches to its remaining task.

After branching, but before commencing the final task, the high and low temperature values are stored in the last four bytes of the first row of the MONTH-table. The last task consists of summing time-on counts for each set-point thermometer over the past 24-hour period. Starting at the beginning of the BASE table, pointed to by the HL registers, and using register C as a count down register, the sum is accumulated in the 16-bit DE register. Thermometer No. 7 is counted on the first time through the SETP loop with subsequent passes progressing to thermometer No. 1. As each sum is obtained, it is stored as a two-byte column entry in the first row of the MONTH table beginning with the first column for thermometer No. 7 and progressing to the seventh column for thermometer No. 1: as shown in the memory map (Table 4-1). After the seven sums have been tallied, the program returns to the SCAN routine.

The last subroutine to be described, HOUR, is flowcharted in Fig. 4-6. Since the DAY subroutine may or may not be executed prior to the execution of the HOUR subroutine, it is necessary that the contents of the microprocessor registers always be in the same state on entering the HOUR subroutine. There are only two tasks to be performed in this subroutine. Both tasks serve to reinitialize the various memory registers assigned to the new current hour. The current-temperature count is first loaded into both the high and low temperature registers for the hour in the MONTH table. The second task resets the current-hour registers to zero for each of the seven set-point thermometers in the BASE data table.

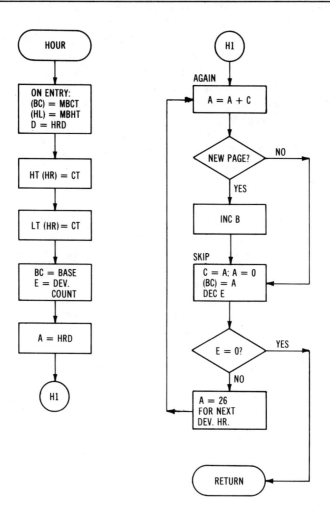

Figure 4-6
HOUR flowchart.

Since the function of the HOUR subroutine is to clear the current-hour entries in the data tables, it should now be apparent why, on the midnight hour, it is necessary to tally the DAY summary before calling the HOUR subroutine.

Summary

The assembly language program described performs the following operations:
1. Initializes the system and enables the interrupt.
2. Services a once-per-second interrupt which displays the time of day of a 24-hour clock.
3. Measures eight thermometric elements once every 15 seconds.
4. Manages a 24-hour data table and a 32-day data table of times and temperatures.

BASIC Utility Programs

Chapter 5

In this chapter, we will consider examples of various programs that can be run in BASIC as background programs while the time and temperature (TNT) machine language program operates in the foreground. In particular, our discussion will cover routines to initialize the data tables, calibrate the thermometers, display the data either in tables or graphically as histograms, save the data on cassette tape, and modify the data tables.

A few important points must be emphasized when running the interrupt driven TNT program. It is obviously necessary that the computer must be left on all the time. However, peripheral equipment, in particular the video display, needs to be on only when in use. Since the power consumption for the computer is less than 50 watts, this represents a very modest energy overhead. When the clock is running, it may be disabled by pressing the Reset button. Disabling the clock does not stop the clock from continuing to run, it only stops the computer from reading the time once a second (and temperature once every 15 seconds). In order to re-enable or to initialize the clock, Rule 1 must be followed. Once re-enabled, the clock will display the correct time, and the temperature monitoring will resume.

* * * * *

RULE 1. To initialize the Clock, execute the direct commands: SYSTEM (Enter)
/31323 (Enter).

* * * * *

The only time that the clock needs to be disabled is when the cassette player is to be used. Since the interrupt would still be operating if the clock were not disabled, any transfer of data between the computer and the cassette recorder would most likely result in a bad load.

* * * * *

RULE 2. Before reading or recording a cassette tape, disable the Clock by pushing the Reset button.

* * * * *

There is only one other precaution that needs to be taken when using the computer for other purposes if the TNT monitor is running. Because hourly and daily updates of the data tables are made on the hour, that is when the minutes and seconds are all zeros, the interrupt should be enabled (clock display operating) when the hour changes. Otherwise, the TNT monitor will not receive the signal to update the data tables.

* * * * *

RULE 3. Do NOT allow the Clock to be disabled on the change-over of an hour.

* * * * *

TNT Monitor

We have discussed the assembly language program in the preceding chapter and also given the assembler listing in Appendix B. Unless it is to be relocated or modified, the program can be loaded with the BASIC program given in Listing 5-1. This program contains only the few commands necessary to load memory with the bulk being devoted to Data statements. The Data statements in lines 400-960 consist of the consecutive decimal bytes of the TNT machine language program. The first data value in each line equals the sum of the remaining ten data byte values. A single error in the program would prevent it from running correctly. Entering the 570 numbers that form the program can easily lead to at least one error. The BASIC program checks each

```
100 M=31323: FOR I=0TO56: READ S
110 FOR J=0TO9: READ X: POKE M+10*I+J,X
120 S=S-X: NEXT J
130 IF S<>0 THEN 150
140 NEXT I: END
150 PRINT "ERROR IN DATA ON LINE #";400+10*I+J-10
160 END
400 DATA 1311,211,0,219,0,230,112,254,0,194,91
410 DATA 819,122,62,195,50,18,64,33,119,122,34
420 DATA 1408,19,64,237,86,251,195,114,0,245,197
430 DATA 1671,213,229,205,229,122,126,254,48,43,202
440 DATA 1549,152,122,254,53,194,223,122,126,254,49
450 DATA 1698,202,163,122,254,52,202,163,122,195,223
460 DATA 1536,122,126,254,51,202,163,122,254,48,194
470 DATA 1215,223,122,205,6,123,229,33,63,60,151
480 DATA 1106,95,126,230,15,131,95,43,126,230,15
490 DATA 952,131,95,43,43,126,230,15,131,95,43
500 DATA 1221,126,230,15,131,194,222,122,95,43,43
510 DATA 1142,126,230,15,131,95,43,126,230,15,131
520 DATA 2044,197,213,204,253,123,209,193,227,205,220
530 DATA 1764,123,225,225,209,193,241,251,201,33,63
540 DATA 925,60,211,0,219,0,79,230,112,7,7
550 DATA 929,7,7,47,60,133,111,121,230,15,198
560 DATA 1373,48,119,125,254,63,194,229,122,219,0
570 DATA 791,201,1,168,124,22,0,33,56,60,126
580 DATA 1315,230,15,254,0,202,34,123,254,1,202
590 DATA 616,32,123,22,20,195,34,123,22,10,35
600 DATA 1215,126,230,15,198,2,130,87,213,197,17
610 DATA 801,0,0,33,144,124,211,1,14,255,19
620 DATA 1114,219,1,169,202,54,123,119,35,71,121
630 DATA 920,47,168,47,79,115,35,114,35,151,129
640 DATA 988,19,19,19,194,54,123,193,209,30,128
650 DATA 985,33,144,124,126,35,35,35,163,202,88
660 DATA 1230,123,213,43,86,43,94,235,209,123,61
670 DATA 1347,202,149,123,197,3,10,188,218,134,123
680 DATA 1247,11,194,124,123,10,189,218,134,123,121
690 DATA 942,130,79,210,131,123,4,10,60,2,193
700 DATA 913,62,26,129,210,142,123,4,79,123,15
710 DATA 876,95,195,85,123,125,2,3,124,2,122
720 DATA 976,214,2,7,7,198,2,129,111,96,210
730 DATA 1456,168,123,36,10,190,218,185,123,194,209
740 DATA 957,123,43,11,10,190,35,3,210,209,123
750 DATA 1057,35,35,10,190,218,200,123,192,43,11
760 DATA 639,10,190,35,3,208,10,119,43,11,10
770 DATA 670,119,35,3,201,10,119,43,11,10,119
780 DATA 643,3,35,35,35,201,10,119,43,43,119
790 DATA 673,11,35,10,119,43,43,119,1,168,124
800 DATA 1098,30,7,122,129,210,243,123,4,79,151
810 DATA 1163,2,29,200,62,26,195,238,123,33,255
820 DATA 697,127,1,237,127,17,46,2,10,119,11
830 DATA 949,43,27,123,178,194,6,124,33,96,125
840 DATA 763,78,35,70,35,94,35,86,62,23,245
850 DATA 1138,35,35,126,184,218,52,124,194,46,124
860 DATA 1023,43,126,185,35,218,52,124,126,71,43
870 DATA 1033,126,79,35,35,35,126,186,218,69,124
880 DATA 1193,194,75,124,43,126,187,35,210,75,124
890 DATA 1036,126,87,43,126,95,35,241,61,194,28
900 DATA 1016,124,62,15,133,111,210,88,124,36,113
910 DATA 777,35,112,35,115,35,114,33,168,124,6
920 DATA 389,7,35,35,14,24,17,0,0,126,131
930 DATA 1036,95,210,114,124,20,35,13,194,107,124
940 DATA 1362,229,33,206,125,125,144,210,129,124,37
950 DATA 1249,144,210,134,124,37,111,115,35,114,225
960 DATA 624,5,194,100,124,201,0,0,0,0,0
```

Listing 5-1. TNT Monitor

line for a possible typographical error. Although the checksum method of error detection is not infallible, it does significantly increase the chance of a correct load. If an incorrect sum is evaluated, the program ends and prints the line number where the error was detected. Before entering this program, the memory size of the computer must be set to reserve memory space for the TNT monitor program.

* * * * *

RULE 4. To reserve space for the TNT monitor program set MEM SIZE = 31322.

* * * * *

Once a successful load is obtained this program should be saved on cassette as a backup.

On execution, the program would attempt to read the time and temperature as it is currently loaded. The temperature reading routine can be disabled until the clock routine is checked out by issuing the direct commands:

POKE 31358,195 (Enter);
POKE 31359,223 (Enter);
POKE 31360,122 (Enter).

This will prevent execution of all of the TNT program except the CLOCK subroutine. The clock can now be started by following Rule 1. The time can be set using the Reset, Slow, and Fast buttons on the interface board.

Once the clock has been checked out and both hardware and software perform satisfactorily, the clock should be disabled (Rule 2), and the TNT monitor restored by issuing the following direct commands:

POKE 31358,126 (Enter);
POKE 31359,254 (Enter);
POKE 31360,48 (Enter).

If the thermometers have not been connected to the interface, they should be connected before re-enabling the clock (Rule 1). If QDT elements are used and not all units are to be used, a jumper wire can be used to short the terminals. For unused thermistor elements, the jumper should be a fixed resistor of about 10K resistance.

* * * * *

RULE 5. ALL thermometer terminals must have a completed circuit for the system to operate.

* * * * *

Thermometer Calibration

We noted in Chapter 2 that each QDT (or thermistor) will have a unique curve relating the duration of the monostable pulse to the temperature, that is the t versus T curve. To determine this relationship, it is necessary to perform the following three operations: 1) Measure t with the computer and interface at several temperatures over a sufficiently broad temperature range. 2) Obtain a "fit" of these data to some particular form of an equation that will yield a set of coefficients. 3) Apply these coefficients to calculate the temperature (T) when given a time count (t).

In addition to the unique dependence of the thermometer element, it is also important to recognize that the other elements in the monostable circuit will also affect the calibration. Thus the resistor in the QDT network and the capacitor in either the thermistor or QDT network have values that may vary as much as 10% greater or lesser than their rated values. As a consequence, the observed time counts obtained in calibrating a thermometer will also depend on the particular capacitor (and resistor) used.

* * * * *

RULE 6. The calibration coefficients obtained for a particular thermometer element are valid only for the specific components used in the calibration.

* * * * *

The TNT monitor uses only the thermometer element wired to data bus line D0 for actual conversion to temperature in degrees. The remaining seven elements are used for set-point measurements. Therefore, only thermometer No. 1 needs to be calibrated. We shall postpone discussion of standardizing the set points for thermometers No. 2-8 to the section on Initialization Routines. The BASIC program used for calibrating the thermometer elements is given in Listing 5-2. The program can be used to calibrate between one and eight elements at the same time. Although it may prove to be somewhat cumbersome to work with all eight elements at one time, four can be conveniently handled. The only reason for calibrating more than one element is to provide for future modifications to your system since the calibration experiment is no more time consuming for several elements than it is for one element.

```
10 DEFDBL X,Y,Z: DIM T(15),X(15),Y(15),Z(3,7),CT(15,8)
100 CLS: PRINT: PRINT TAB(12)"THERMOMETER CALIBRATION": PRINT
110 PRINT "OPTION #1 - DATA ACQUISITION EXPERIMENT"
120 PRINT "OPTION #2 - CREATE DATA STATEMENTS"
130 PRINT "OPTION #3 - READ DATA STATEMENTS"
140 PRINT "OPTION #4 - LINEAR CURVE FIT (THERMISTOR)"
150 PRINT "OPTION #5 - PARABOLIC CURVE FIT (QUAD DIODE)"
160 PRINT "OPTION #6 - COMPARISON OF CALCULATED RESULTS"
170 PRINT "OPTION #7 - COUNT TO TEMPERATURE CONVERTER"
180 PRINT "OPTION #8 - TEMPERATURE TO COUNT CONVERTER"
190 PRINT "OPTION #9 - READ THERMOMETER COUNTS"
200 PRINT: PRINT TAB(12)"";: INPUT "SELECT OPTION #";A
210 IF A>9 THEN 200
220 ON A GOTO 1000,2000,3000,4000,5000,6000,7000,8000,9000
230 GOTO 200
1000 INPUT "HOW MANY THERMOMETERS";N
1010 CLS: PRINT@0,"THERM:";: FOR J=1 TO N
1020 PRINT@J*6," #"J;: NEXT J
1030 FOR J=1 TO 15: PRINT@951,"T";: INPUT T(J)
1040 T(J)=(9*T(J)/5)+32
1050 PRINT@951,"         ";: PRINT@J*64,T(J);
1060 FOR I=31888 TO 31910 STEP 3
1070 K=1+LOG(PEEK(I))/LOG(2): X=PEEK(I+1): Y=PEEK(I+2)
1080 CT(J,K)=X+256*Y
1090 PRINT@6+J*64+6*(K-1),CT(J,K);: NEXT I: NEXT J
1100 PRINT@1016,"DONE";
1110 A$=INKEY$: IF A$="" THEN 1110 ELSE 100
2000 CLS: PRINT "TYPE /EACH DATA SET/ INTO A DATA STATEMENT"
2010 FOR J=1 TO 15: PRINT T(J);: NEXT J: PRINT "/";
2020 FOR K=1 TO N: FOR J=1 TO 15: PRINT CT(J,K);
2030 NEXT J: PRINT "/";:   NEXT K
2040 PRINT: AUTO 10000
3000 FOR J=1 TO 15: READ T(J): NEXT J
3010 IF N=0 THEN INPUT "HOW MANY THERMOMETERS";N
3020 FOR K=1 TO N: FOR J=1 TO 15: READ CT(J,K): NEXT J: NEXT K
3030 CLS: PRINT: FOR J=1 TO 15: PRINT T(J);: FOR K=1 TO N
3040 PRINT TAB(7*K) CT(J,K);: NEXT K: PRINT: NEXT J: RESTORE
3050 A$=INKEY$: IF A$="" THEN 3050 ELSE 100
```

Listing 5-2. Thermometer Calibration, Part 1

Data Acquisition

Lines 1000 through 1090 are used to obtain 15 sets of data. With the TNT foreground program running, this background program reads the BUF table to obtain the counts of all eight elements taken in the most recent 15-second interval. Recall that the BUF table holds these counts in memory locations 31888-31911 using three consecutive bytes to store the thermometer code and the low and high value bytes of the count, respectively. The byte that stores the thermometer code is stored with zero in all bits except the bit of the data bus line connected to the output of that thermometer. When these codes are read by the BASIC program, the numbers corresponding to D0 through D7, respectively, are 1, 2, 4, 8, 16, 32, 64, and 128. These values are converted to the corresponding thermometer number in line 1070. Recall also that the BUF table is organized from the shortest count to the longest count. Although the program acquires and displays all eight thermometer counts, only the number requested will have coefficients computed.

The thermometer counts are read by the program and assigned to the CT(J,K) table only after a temperature has been input. Obtaining the temperatures which provide the calibration data for the thermometer element(s) is probably the single most important part of the entire process. The first requirement is the need for a quality mercury-in-glass thermometer having its scale engraved in the glass stem of the thermometer. This type of thermometer is typically used in high school and college chemistry and physics laboratory classes. They are approximately 12 inches long and require about 3 inches immersion. Generally they will be marked in the Celsius scale between $-20°$ and $+110°$, although Fahrenheit thermometers are available. Each degree interval is engraved and measures slightly less than 1/16th inch—large enough to estimate to a tenth of a degree. They are available from scientific laboratory supply houses and cost around $5.00. More than likely, you may be able to borrow one from a local high school or college science department.

To obtain a good calibration curve, the temperature range should extend over the same range that you anticipate will be used in your measurements. By doing this, your measurements will always lie between two calibration points. This is known as interpolation. Calculating much beyond the calibration range (extrapolation) can lead to very large errors. For an outdoor thermometer, a minimum range for 0°F (-18°C) to 120°F (49°C) is adequate for most geographical regions. Although the lower end of this range may be somewhat higher than desirable, it is a good compromise for two reasons. First, as we have already noted, the lowest temperature of the calibration thermometer is commonly -20°C. Secondly, this range is easily duplicated in a home experiment since food freezers are set near 0°F.

The equipment required for the calibration experiment consists of the set of thermometer elements with their requisite lead lengths attached, a small thermos bottle (preferably of half-pint volume and having a narrow mouth), the glass thermometer, and a pint of isopropyl rubbing alcohol (70% by volume) available from any drug store (preferably in a plastic container). The first step in the experiment is to standardize the glass thermometer by filling the thermos with cracked ice and clean water. Immerse the glass thermometer and gently (!) stir this mixture and record the equilibrated temperature. It should read 0.0°C. If it does not, all subsequent thermometer readings should be corrected by adding (if below 0°) or subtracting (if above 0°) this value.

After you have standardized the glass thermometer, the rest of the experiment may be performed in two parts consisting of a set of temperatures taken below room temperature and a set taken above room temperature. The thermometer elements should be attached to the immersion end of the glass thermometer with a couple of rubber bands such that the elements cluster around the bulb of the thermometer but that the leads do not obstruct the engraved stem of the thermometer. A spring clip clothespin can be used to support this assembly about an inch above the bottom of the thermos. The easiest way to proceed with the low temperature part of the experiment is to *chill the thermos* containing 4 oz. (one-half cup) of rubbing alcohol in the food freezer for several hours. *Warm the bottle* of alcohol to about 100°F (slightly above body temperature) under hot tap water and store the bottle in a bowl filled with hot water. Start the BASIC program and before inserting the thermometer assembly into the thermos, obtain a reading at room temperature as the first point.

Then, insert the thermometer assembly into the thermos with the clothespin resting on its mouth, and gently (!) stir. As soon as the thermometer has reached its lowest temperature and remained constant for a minute, enter the temperature reading into the computer. The program, as given in the listing, expects a Celsius reading but converts it to Fahrenheit in line 1040. If your thermometer is already in Fahrenheit, delete line 1040 before running the program. To raise the temperature to higher equilibrium (steady) values at about 8 Fahrenheit degree (4.4 Celsius degree) intervals, add 1/2 oz. (1 measured tablespoon) of warm alcohol to the thermos. You will need about 10 readings in the cold range.

For the first 4 or 5 points, 1/2 oz. increments will provide a large enough temperature change. After this you will have to add 1 oz. increments to change the temperature significantly. Also after 3 or 3.5 oz. have been added, the thermos will be nearly full. Empty the contents into a measuring cup and return only 4 oz. of the

Table 5–1. Temperature Adjustment Schedule for Calibration Experiment

Data Point #	Initial Temp. T1, deg. F	Initial Volume V1, oz.	Volume Added V2, oz. at T2 = 100°F	Final Temp. T, deg. F
1	75	-	-	-
2	0	4.0	0.5	10
3	10	4.5	0.5	18
4	18	5.0	0.5.	25
5	25	5.5	0.5	31
6	31	6.0	1.0	40
7	40	7.0	1.0	47
8	47	4.0 (!)	1.0	56
9	56	5.0	1.0	62
10	62	6.0	1.0	67
11	67	7.0	-	-
			V2, oz. at T2 = 32°F	
12	120	4.0	0.5	111
13	111	4.5	0.5	104
14	104	5.0	1.0	82
15	82	6.0	-	-

cold alcohol to the thermos. Table 5-1 lists the theoretical temperatures for both the cold range and the hot range (see the next equation) calibration runs, assuming exact quantities and temperatures. You should not expect to duplicate these figures but they can serve as a guide. The heat balance equation used to calculate the table is

$$(V1 + V2)(T - T1) = V2(T2 - T)$$

where V2 is the volume of alcohol at temperature T2 which is added to the volume V1 in the thermos at temperature T1 to yield the combined volume (V1 + V2) at the new temperature T.

To obtain the high temperature points, preheat 4 oz. of alcohol by warming (with continuous shaking) in a pan of water heated over an electric element. When the temperature of the alcohol is about 125°F, transfer the alcohol to the thermos. Chill the bottle of alcohol in a bowl of cold water containing several ice cubes. Obtain the remaining five or six points by successively equilibrating by gently stirring with the thermometer assembly, entering the temperature into the program, then lowering to a new temperature about 10 Fahrenheit degrees (5.5 Celsius degrees) cooler and re-equilibrating.

This process should not be rushed, otherwise false readings will be obtained and an invalid calibration will result. It cannot be overemphasized that constant and gentle stirring of the liquid in the thermos is absolutely required to achieve true equilibrium temperatures. Temperature layers in the liquid can result with the elements not being at the precise temperature of the glass thermometer bulb. if data of this type is obtained, there will be considerable scatter of the calibration points about the computed curve, resulting in considerable error (uncertainty) in the values of the coefficients. Although the process is tedious, excellent results can be obtained with a little care. As a rough guide, it should take between 5 and 10 minutes to readjust to each new temperature. There is nothing to be gained by trying to make each temperature interval exact. The aim should rather be to distribute the 15 temperatures so that they are reasonably spaced over the entire range. Tables 5-2 and 5-3 list the experimental and calculated results obtained for a thermistor and a QDT calibration. As a precaution, it is advisable to write the data down on paper as it is obtained in case a problem develops during the experiment. As we shall see, it is a simple matter to revise the program to accept data separately from the experiment.

Once both parts of the experiment have been completed, the data will remain on the video screen until any key is pressed. Pressing a key will display the Option List. At this point, the data are stored as variables and the curve-fitting calculations could be performed. However, it is a safer move to create Data Statements and save the data so that it may be read back into the program. Option No. 2 (lines 2000-2050) lists the data on the video screen in the format in which it should be saved; and then executes an Auto command. Since this is a direct command, you will exit the program and be put into program line creation mode with line number 10000. Lines beginning at 10000 are reserved for Data statements. The format is to enter all temperatures in the first data statements with each subsequent line holding the 15 counts of one element in the same order as the temperatures. Listing 5-3 illustrates this format for one element. After the Data

```
10000 DATA 1.4,12.2,21.2,27.5,32.9,35.6,40.46,51.62,60.62,69.98,78.8,89.78,10
      2.02,106.34,122
10010 DATA 11031,8364,6680,5724,5160,5049,4574,3784,3350,2941,2671,2379,2120,
      2033,1807
10020 'DATA 2.12,8.6,15.26,21.2,26.6,33.8,42.8,49.82,55.58,62.42,78.8,94.64,1
      03.82,111.2,117.5
10030 'DATA 25444,20596,16512,13824,11676,9272,7101,5816,4925,4094.2705,1830,
      1472,1161,987
```

Listing 5-3. Sample Data Statements

Statements have been created, on executing the program with a RUN command, it will be necessary to Read the data back into the program using Option No. 3 (lines 3000-3050). This completes the data acquisition part of the Calibration program.

Curve Fitting

The second part of this program is provided in Listing 5-4. This part covers the curve-fitting calculations required to obtain the set of coefficients. Option No. 4 (lines 4000-4170) and Option No. 5 (lines 5000-5370) are separate routines used to perform linear least squares analyses of a straight line function and a curved

Table 5–2. Thermistor Calibration Data and Results

Log(CT) = (7430.01/T) + (− 5.92226)					
T(MEAS.)	CT(MEAS.)	CT(CALC.)	T(CALC.)	T(M) − T(C)	RMS T
2.12	25444	26011	2.75	− 0.6	0.98
8.60	20596	20819	8.92	− 0.3	
15.26	16512	16666	15.54	− 0.3	
21.20	13824	13738	21.01	0.2	
26.60	11676	11572	26.32	0.3	
33.80	9272	9260	33.76	0.0	
42.80	7101	7071	42.66	0.1	
49.82	5816	5768	49.53	0.3	
55.58	4925	4900	55.40	0.2	
62.42	4094	4057	62.09	0.3	
78.80	2705	2631	77.73	1.1	
94.64	1830	1774	93.36	1.3	
103.82	1472	1424	102.47	1.3	
111.20	1161	1202	112.75	− 1.6	
117.50	987	1043	120.00	− 2.5	

Log(CT) = (− 695717/T²) + (10132.1/T) + (− 8.53247)					
T(MEAS.)	CT(MEAS.)	CT(CALC.)	T(CALC.)	T(M) − T(C)	RMS T
2.12	25444	25463	2.14	0.0	0.75
8.60	20596	20559	8.55	0.0	
15.26	16512	16581	15.39	− 0.1	
21.20	13824	13742	21.01	0.2	
26.60	11676	11622	26.45	− 0.1	
33.80	9272	9339	34.04	− 0.2	
42.80	7101	7155	43.06	− 0.3	
49.82	5816	5844	49.99	− 0.2	
55.58	4925	4966	55.88	− 0.3	
62.42	4094	4109	62.56	− 0.2	
78.80	2705	2653	78.07	0.7	
94.64	1830	1774	93.40	1.2	
103.82	1472	1417	102.26	1.5	
111.20	1161	1188	112.20	− 1.0	
117.50	987	1025	119.16	− 1.7	

Table 5–2 cont.

Log(CT) = $(-1.81727E + 11/T^4) + (3.29598E + 06/T^2) + (-1.32305)$					
T(MEAS.)	CT(MEAS.)	CT(CALC.)	T(CALC)	T(M) – T(C)	RMS T
2.12	25444	25229	1.86	0.3	0.81
8.60	20596	20488	8.44	0.2	
15.26	16512	16590	15.41	– 0.1	
21.20	13824	13781	21.10	0.1	
26.60	11676	11669	26.58	0.0	
33.80	9272	9382	34.19	– 0.4	
42.80	7101	7185	43.20	– 0.4	
49.82	5816	5863	50.10	– 0.3	
55.58	4925	4977	55.96	– 0.4	
62.42	4094	4113	62.60	– 0.2	
78.80	2705	2649	78.00	0.8	
94.64	1830	1769	93.28	1.4	
103.82	1472	1413	102.15	1.7	
111.20	1161	1186	112.13	– 0.9	
117.50	987	1025	119.17	– 1.7	

function, respectively. Without delving into the mathematical (or statistical) justification, we can note that a least squares analysis of data is a very practical and efficient means of obtaining a unique set of coefficients to represent a smooth relationship between a dependent and an independent variable. Specifically, the least squares analysis determines the coefficients of a mathematical equation by selecting the (only) curve for which the experimental data points have the smallest (least) value for the sum of the squares of the deviations of its points. The deviation of a point is the displacement of the data point along the direction of the dependent variable (the y, or vertical, axis by convention) from the curve at the value of the point's independent variable (the x, or horizontal, axis conventionally).

There will always be some deviation (or scatter) of the experimental points about a smooth curve due to random fluctuations that are always present in an experiment: this is the equivalent of noise. The primary objective in curve fitting is to choose an appropriate mathematical function to fit to the data. Note especially that there is no way to know beforehand the

Table 5–3. Quad Diode Thermometer Calibration Data and Results

Log(CT) = (3938.02/T) + (0.612493)					
T(MEAS.)	CT(MEAS.)	CT(CALC.)	T(CALC.)	T(M) – T(C)	RMS T
1.40	11031	9442	– 6.84	8.2	4.6
12.20	8364	7766	8.04	4.2	
21.20	6680	6643	20.88	0.3	
27.50	5724	5975	30.11	– 2.6	
32.90	5160	5468	36.51	– 3.6	
35.60	5049	5235	37.87	– 2.3	
40.46	4574	4846	44.16	– 3.7	
51.62	3784	4081	56.69	– 5.1	
60.62	3350	3572	65.07	– 4.4	
69.98	2941	3125	74.34	– 4.4	
78.80	2671	2766	81.41	– 2.6	
89.78	2379	2390	90.15	– 0.4	
102.02	2120	2044	99.15	2.9	
106.34	2033	1938	102.49	3.9	
122.00	1807	1607	112.11	9.9	

Log(CT) = (4.20031E + 06/T²) + (– 12349.2/T) + (16.3276)					
T(MEAS.)	CT(MEAS.)	CT(CALC.)	T(CALC.)	T(M) – T(C)	RMS T
1.40	11031	10951	1.14	0.3	0.81
12.20	8364	8268	11.73	0.5	
21.20	6680	6704	21.37	– 0.2	
27.50	5724	5860	28.65	– 1.2	
32.90	5160	5260	33.90	– 1.0	
35.60	5049	4996	35.04	0.6	
40.46	4574	4571	40.43	0.0	
51.62	3784	3795	51.81	– 0.2	
60.62	3350	3322	60.02	0.6	
69.98	2941	2934	69.80	0.2	
78.80	2671	2643	77.87	0.9	
89.78	2379	2356	88.80	1.0	
102.02	2120	2111	101.51	0.5	
106.34	2033	2039	106.73	– 0.4	
122.00	1807	1828	123.95	2.0	

Table 5–3 cont.

Log(CT) = (2.09078E + 11/T⁴) + (− 570194/T²) + (7.36386)					
T(MEAS.)	CT(MEAS.)	CT(CALC.)	T(CALC.)	T(M) − T(C)	RMS T
1.40	11031	11016	1.36	0.0	0.54
12.20	8364	8262	11.71	0.5	
21.20	6680	6684	21.23	0.0	
27.50	5724	5840	28.48	− 1.0	
32.90	5160	5244	33.74	− 0.8	
35.60	5049	4982	34.89	0.7	
40.46	4574	4561	40.31	0.1	
51.62	3784	3795	51.82	− 0.2	
60.62	3350	3328	60.15	0.5	
69.98	2941	2944	70.08	− 0.1	
78.80	2671	2654	78.24	0.6	
89.78	2379	2365	89.21	0.6	
102.02	2120	2114	101.74	0.3	
106.34	2033	2040	106.79	− 0.4	
122.00	1807	1816	122.80	− 0.8	

specific function which will give the best empirical representation. There are some guidelines, however, that can be used to select the function.

The simplest relationship between two variables, say x and y, is one representing a straight line. The equation for a straight line is

$$y = Ax + B$$

where A is the slope of the line, that is how much y changes per unit change in x (or the "rise" divided by the "run"), and B is the intercept or the value of y when $x = 0$. A very common relationship (with theoretical physico-chemical justification) between many physical properties that are dependent variables of temperature as an independent variable is given by the equation

$$\log t = \frac{A}{T} + B$$

```
4000 REM LEAST SQUARES OF Y = A*X + B
4010 FOR K=1 TO N
4020 CLS: PRINT "CALCULATING LOG(CT)=A/T+B"
4030 XS=0: YS=0: XX=0: XY=0: YY=0
4040 FOR I=1 TO 15: X(I)=1/(T(I)+459.7): Y(I)=LOG(CT(I,K))
4050 XS=XS+X(I): YS=YS+Y(I)
4060 XY=XY+X(I)*Y(I):XX=XX+X(I)*X(I)
4070 NEXT I
4080 XN=(15*XY)-(XS*YS): XM=(XX*YS)-(XS*XY)
4090 XD=(15*XX)-(XS*XS)
4100 A(K)=XN/XD: B(K)=XM/XD
4110 NEXT K
4120 CLS: PRINT "WRITE DOWN THESE COEFFICIENTS"
4130 PRINT"THERM.","A(T↑-1)","B"
4140 FOR K=1 TO N
4150 PRINT "#"K,A(K),B(K): NEXT K
4160 PRINT: PRINT "PRESS ANY KEY TO RETURN TO OPTION LIST"
4170 A$=INKEY$: IF A$="" THEN 4170 ELSE 100
5000 REM LEAST SQUARES OF Y = A*X↑2 + B*X + C
5010 FOR K=1 TO N
5020 CLS: PRINT "CALCULATING LOG(CT)=A/T↑4+B/T↑2+C"
5030 YS=0: YX=0: Y2=0: XY=0: XS=0: X2=0: X3=0: X4=0
5040 FOR I=1 TO 15
5050 X(I)=459.7+T(I): X(I)=1/(X(I)*X(I)): Y(I)=LOG(CT(I,K))
5060 XS=XS+X(I):X2=X2+(X(I)↑2):X3=X3+(X(I)↑3):X4=X4+(X(I)↑4)
5070 YS=YS+Y(I):Y2=Y2+Y(I)↑2:YX=YX+Y(I)*X(I):XY=XY+Y(I)*X(I)↑2
5080 NEXT I
5090 FOR R=1 TO 3: FOR C=1 TO 7: Z(R,C)=0: NEXT C: NEXT R
5100 FOR R=1 TO 3: FOR C=1 TO 3
5110 ON R+C-2 GOTO 5130,5140,5150,5160
5120 Z(R,C)=15: GOTO 5170
5130 Z(R,C)=XS: GOTO 5170
5140 Z(R,C)=X2: GOTO 5170
5150 Z(R,C)=X3: GOTO 5170
5160 Z(R,C)=X4
5170 NEXT C: NEXT R
5180 Z(1,4)=YS: Z(2,4)=YX: Z(3,4)=XY
5190 FOR C=5 TO 7: R=C-4: Z(R,C)=1: NEXT C
5200 FOR R=1 TO 3: GOSUB 5300: NEXT R
5210 C3(K)=Z(3,4): C2(K)=Z(2,4): C1(K)=Z(1,4)
5230 NEXT K
5240 CLS: PRINT "WRITE DOWN THESE COEFFICIENTS"
5250 PRINT "THERM.","A(T↑-4)","B(I↑-2)","C"
5260 FOR K=1 TO N
5270 PRINT "#"K,C3(K),C2(K),C1(K): NEXT K
5280 PRINT : PRINT "PRESS ANY KEY TO RETURN TO OPTION LIST"
5290 A$=INKEY$: IF A$="" THEN 5290 ELSE 100
5300 FOR C=R+1 TO 7: Z(R,C)=Z(R,C)/Z(R,R): NEXT C
5310 Z(R,R)=1
5320 FOR I=1 TO 3: FOR C=R+1 TO 7
5330 IF I<>R THEN Z(I,C)=Z(I,C)-Z(I,R)*Z(R,C)
5340 NEXT C: NEXT I
5350 FOR I=1 TO 3
5360 IF I<>R THENZ(I,R)=0
5370 NEXT I: RETURN
```
Listing 5-4 Thermometer Calibration, Part 2

where we make the substitutions

$$y = \log t$$

and

$$x = \frac{1}{T}$$

to obtain a straight line function. This specific relationship often works quite well for empirically fitting the temperature dependence of the resistance of a thermistor. Since the computer measures the duration of the monostable pulse, t, which is directly proportional to the thermistor resistance, that is:

$$t = R \, C \, \log 3 = R \times (\text{constant})$$

we can attempt to calibrate the thermistor according to the expression:

$$\log(t) = \frac{A}{T} + B$$

by evaluating the coefficients A and B from experimentally measured data of t and T.

One of the simpler functions to fit a smooth curve which is not a straight line is based on the equation for a parabola. This is the shape of the trajectory of a cannon ball, a chain suspended between two points, or the cross section of an auto headlight reflector. Its general equation is:

$$2p(y - k) = (x - h)^2$$

where k and h are constants that determine the position of the curve with respect to the origin and p determines how sharply the curve bends. If the implied multiplication is carried out for this equation and the constants are collected, we obtain

$$y = \left(\frac{1}{2p}\right)x^2 + \left(\frac{-h}{p}\right)x + \left(\frac{h^2}{2p}\right) + k$$

which can be written as

$$y = Ax^2 + Bx + C$$

This equation contains three unique coefficients (A, B, C) that can also be determined in a least squares analysis. In general, the straight line and parabolic functions are the first two members of a whole family of functions known as terminated power series. The next possible function contains four coefficients and would be

$$y = Ax^3 + Bx^2 + Cx + D$$

and so forth.

It has been stated (somewhat facetiously) that any set of experimental data that is a function of two variables (x and y) can be fitted to any curve if enough coefficients (and powers of x) are included. There are two important restrictions to this remark that deserve attention. The first (and simplest) is that there must be at least as many experimental points as the number of coefficients to be determined. As we shall see, this is the identical restriction as found in solving simultaneous equations where there has to be at least as many equations as there are unknowns. Actually, in dealing with curve fitting of experimental data, it can be disastrous, for example, to use only two points to determine the two coefficients of a straight line. Because each point obtained in a physical measurement has an uncertainty associated with it (the noise referred to previously), it is necessary to obtain several points that can (in some manner) be averaged. This averaging tends to cancel the randomness of the individual uncertainties. In general, a minimum of seven points reduces the odds of obtaining spurious results while collecting more than fifteen points does not significantly improve those odds.

The second important restriction of curve fitting is also related to the uncertainty (or random error) associated with a measurement. There comes a point in fitting data to a curve that, although adding an additional coefficient improves the "goodness of fit," it does not improve the fit enough to warrant evaluating (and employing) the additional coefficient. For many measurements, this is the case in selecting the straight-line fit over that of a parabolic fit. There are statistical methods for evaluating these conditions. In particular, the interested reader should refer to the Student t Test and the Fisher F Test concerning the two points discussed here. It is possible, however, to qualitatively decide the goodness of fit of data by examining the residuals of the data with respect to the calculated curve rather than invoking the more sophisticated statistical tests. These residuals are numerically the same as the deviations (displacements) referred to previously in the description of least squares analysis. A residual differs from the deviation by having a plus or minus sign associated with it to indicate whether the data point lies above or below the curve. It can be calculated for any point from the expression:

$$r(i) = y(i) \{ \text{meas.} \} - y(i) <\text{calc.}>$$

but since, for the straight line equation,

$$y(i) <\text{calc.}> = A\, x(i) + B$$

then
$$r(i) = y(i) - A\, x(i) - B$$

Here, the coefficients, A and B, are obtained from the least squares computer program, and x(i) and y(i) represent the pair of values for one measured point.

In examining the data of the thermometer calibration experiment, it is not physically very meaningful to look at the y residuals since they are logarithms of the monostable counts. It is just as confusing to examine the x residuals since they are the reciprocals of the (absolute) temperature. It is far more interesting to calculate the Fahrenheit temperature that the coefficients of the equation predict for each measured monostable count, and compare that calculated temperature to the temperature measured at that count. Referring back to Tables 5-2 and 5-3, the residuals of the Fahrenheit temperatures are listed in the fifth column of each table. There are two observations to be made concerning these. First, the magnitudes of the residuals give an immediate indication of the goodness of fit. For example, look at the three fits in Table 5-3 for the QDT. It is immediately obvious that the straight line fit is very poor compared to the two parabolic fits. A simple means of making this observation more quantitative is to add the squares of all residuals in a column and divide by the number of points (15 in all cases) then take the square root. This is a root mean square (RMS) deviation. The RMS deviation of the straight line fit is 6 times greater than the simpler parabolic fit. The second observation about how well a certain form of equation fits the experimental data is also apparent in this part of Table 5-3.

Note how the residuals systematically change over the temperature span. At 1.4°, the residual is large and positive. With increasing temperature, the residuals get smaller, go to a large negative value at mid-range, and then progressively increase to a large positive value at 122°. This trend is clearly not random and does not indicate poor measurements but rather a poor choice of equation. Only when the residuals fluctuate randomly both in size and direction over the span of a variable can you be reasonably certain that you are seeing experimental uncertainty rather than some systematic error. In this respect, the manner in which you obtain a set of data is also useful in avoiding systematic errors. For example, in the calibration experiment, by taking the room temperature (midpoint) first, and then approaching that point from either side by warming from the low temperature end and cooling from the high temperature end of the range, it is possible to check whether the data are converging. *No amount of statistical calculations can improve poor data!*

Three different functions have been fitted to the calibration data in Tables 5-2 and 5-3. In all three cases, the dependent variable is chosen as the (natural) logarithm of the count time of the monostable pulse. In the first two cases, the independent variable was chosen as the reciprocal of the (absolute) temperature, while in the third case, the square of the reciprocal temperature was taken as the independent variable. We have chosen to refer our temperatures to the Fahrenheit scale because it is more familiar and also because it provides almost twice (1.8) the precision when working with integer values. When performing curve-fitting calculations, the math is considerably simplified by working only with positive temperatures. In fact, in terms of the fundamental properties of materials, only positive temperatures are physically meaningful. As you may know, there exists a temperature, known as absolute zero, that represents the lowest (coldest) limit of temperature. This point lies 459.7° below 0°F. Therefore, by converting the experimental data to the absolute Fahrenheit scale, our calculations for curve fitting become manageable. Both Options No. 4 and No. 5 convert the temperatures to absolute before performing the least squares analysis and then reconvert the results back to the ordinary (relative) Fahrenheit scale for tabulation.

The selection of $x = (1/T)^2$ for the third fit is purely empirical because it was determined that QDTs gave better calibration results. The rms T in Table 5-3 shows a 50% improvement over the other parabolic fit with $x = 1/T$. This choice of the independent variable still requires only three coefficients and is only a matter of the choice of a different variable. It is not the same as computing an additional coefficient. Option No. 5 of the program is set up for performing the parabolic fit using this variable. However, in order to perform a parabolic least squares fit versus $(1/T)$ only requires that line 5050 be altered to set $X(I) = 1/X(I)$ instead of $1/[X(I)*X(I)]$.

It has been stated that once the coefficients have been obtained, absurd results can be obtained for calculations made outside the calibration range. As an example, consider the parabolic and straight line fits of log t versus $1/T$ for the QDT in Table 5-3. These data and the curves obtained from the calculated coefficients are plotted in Fig. 5-1. The data is intentionally compressed in this figure to illustrate the graphical meaning of the various coefficients obtained. The scale of the horizontal axis has been adjusted in order to make a unit in the vertical dimension $(y = \log t)$ equal to a unit in the horizontal dimension $[x = 5000/T,$ with $T = T(F) + 459.7]$. This adjustment is necessary in order to show the parabolic curve without distortion. The first thing to be noted about a plot in $1/T$ is that the actual temperature decreases from left to right. Whereas absolute zero $(-459.7°F)$ lies infinitely far to the right, infinite temperature corresponds to the origin where $1/T = 0$.

Consider the straight-line fit. Starting in the lower left corner of the graph near the origin, the coefficient B, equal to 0.612, is the intercept or value of $y = \log t$ when x is zero. The line rises at a rate given by the coefficient A, equal to 0.788 per unit of $5000/T$. Our earlier discussion of the poorness of this fit becomes immediately apparent as the line crosses the region of the data points. The obvious curvature of the data which the line intersects shows positive deviations at either end of the arc and negative deviations in the center.

In considering the parabolic fit, there are several interesting points to be noted. The C coefficient is the intercept. The point at

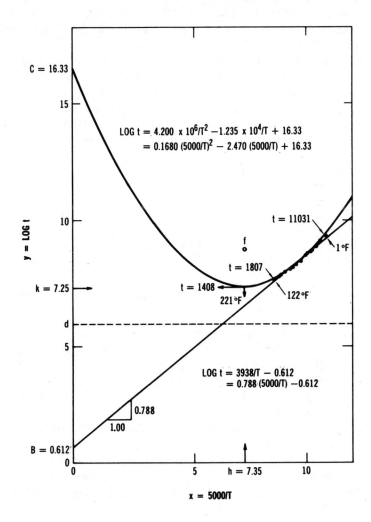

Figure 5-1
Least squares calibration curves.

$x = h$ and $y = k$ is called the *vertex* of the parabola. The curve is symmetric about this point and rises on either side with the same shape. The amount of curvature of the parabola is determined by the point f, called the *focus* or *focal point*, and the line d, known as the *directrix*. The distance of any point on the curve to the focus is equal to the vertical distance from that point to the directrix. Thus, at the value of $x = h$, the directrix lies as far below the bottom (vertex) as the focal point lies above. What is more, the vertical distance between f and d is equal to the horizontal distance from f to the curve to either side of f. All of these distances are related to the parameter p given in the general equation for the parabola at the beginning of this section. The three parameters, h, k, and p, can be calculated from the least squares coefficients by the following set of equations:

$$p = \frac{1}{2A} = \frac{1}{2(0.1680)} = 2.98$$

$$h = \frac{-B}{2A} = \frac{2.470}{2(0.1680)} = 7.35$$

$$k = C - \left(\frac{B^2}{4A}\right) = 16.33 - \left[\frac{(2.470)^2}{4(0.1680)}\right] = 7.25$$

We have dwelt on these properties of the parabola in order to emphasize the dangers of misusing the calibration curve. It is obvious that the curve for this particular QDT predicts that the count time goes to a minimum value: at $\log t = 7.25$ ($t = 1408$) and a temperature of 221°F. On the other hand, the straight-line calibration predicts no such limiting value. In all likelihood, both of these curves are wrong in their predictions because we are extrapolating too far beyond the range of calibration. When a thermometer element is fitted to a parabolic equation, the calculation of the vertex point is a convenient method of ascertaining the maximum range before absurd results will be obtained.

We conclude this section with some general comments about the least squares calculations. Up to this point, we have assumed that we can obtain a set of coefficients that can be used to convert a count time, t (labeled CT in the computer program), to its equivalent temperature. Two important points have been made. First, the choice of the form of the equation must be made on grounds independent of the least squares analysis. Second, the least squares analysis will provide a unique set of coefficients of the preselected equation based on the criterion of minimization of the sum of the squares of the residuals. At first glance, the analysis appears to be performed backwards. We start with a set of x,y data pairs and want to calculate the "constants" (coefficients) of an equation. It turns out that for any selected equation of N terms (and N coefficients), one can generate a set of N simultaneous equations which have to be solved for the coefficients (the unknowns). As we have noted, the "knowns" are the set of x's and y's. For example, suppose we wish to fit a parabolic equation. There are three coefficients: therefore we need three equations. These equations are generated in the following steps:

1. Write down the general equation:

$$y = Ax^2 + Bx + C$$

2. Write down a second equation obtained by multiplying both sides of the general equation by the independent variable as it appears in one of the terms in the general equation, let's take the Bx term—then we want to multiply through by "x":

$$xy = Ax^3 + Bx^2 + Cx$$

3. Repeat Step 2 for each additional term in the general equation. In our example, there is only one additional term, namely the Ax^2 term, so we multiply through by x^2:

$$x^2y = Ax^4 + Bx^3 + Cx^2$$

4. For each term in the equations, substitute the sum of all the experimental data points. For example, for x^2, calculate the squares of all the x data values and add them together. Denote this as $S(x^2) = x(1)^2 + x(2)^2 + \ldots + x(N)^2$, where N is the number of points. Note particularly, that this is the sum of the squares NOT the square of the sum!

5. Simultaneously solve the set of equations:

$$S(y) = A\ S(x^2) + B\ S(x) + C\ N$$

$$S(xy) = A\ S(x^3) + B\ S(x^2) + C\ S(x)$$

$$S(x^2y) = A\ S(x^4) + B\ S(x^3) + C\ S(x^2)$$

where all S( ) terms are numbers. Note that in the first equation, when C is summed over all data points, we obtain $S(C) = C(1) + C(2) + \ldots + C(N) = N\ C$.

Before we mention how the program solves these equations, let's apply these rules to the equation for a straight line.

Step 1. $y = A\ x + B$
Step 2. $xy = A\ x^2 + B\ x$
Step 3. Not required—all independent terms are accounted for.
Step 4. $S(y) = A\ S(x) + B\ N$
$S(xy) = A\ S(x^2) + B\ S(x)$
Step 5. Since two equations in two unknowns are easy to solve, we obtain:

$$A = \frac{[N\ S(xy) - S(x)\ S(y)]}{[N\ S(x^2) - S(x)^2]}$$

$$B = \frac{[S(x^2)\ S(y) - S(x)\ S(xy)]}{[N\ S(x^2) - S(x)^2]}$$

Note that the second term in the denominator of both equations is the square of the sum of x's NOT the sum of the squares of x's! If you refer back to Listing 5-4, you will find this solution in lines 4080-4100 of Option No. 4. The sums of the various powers and products are calculated in the loop at lines 4040 through 4070.

Now let's return to solving three (or more) simultaneous equations. This is the situation in Option No. 5. The details of this calculation are tedious, to say the least. Suffice it to say that the algorithm used by the computer program systematically divides, multiplies, adds, and subtracts various terms in order to reduce the original three equations from the form:

$$N\ C + S(x)\ B + S(x^2)\ A = S(y)$$

$$S(x) \, C + S(x^2) \, B + S(x^3) \, A = S(xy)$$

$$S(x^2) \, C + S(x^3) \, B + S(x^4) \, A = S(x^2y)$$

into the following form:

$$1 \, C + 0 \, B + 0 \, A = c$$

$$0 \, C + 1 \, B + 0 \, A = b$$

$$0 \, C + 0 \, B + 1 \, A = a$$

For example, the easiest (and first) step is to reduce the first term of the first equation to one by dividing both sides of the equation by N:

$$1C + \frac{S(x) \, B}{N} + \frac{S(x^2) \, A}{N} = \frac{S(y)}{N}$$

The actual algorithm uses a method of operating on an augmented matrix of the S( ) terms to evaluate the inverse of the matrix. In the program, the elements of the matrix are denoted by Z(R,C), where R and C refer to the row and column indices of a 3 × 7 matrix.

One final word of caution about least squares calculations needs to be mentioned. Ordinarily in calculating with data obtained from physical measurements, a calculated result can never be more precise than the least precise quantity used in the calculation. Specifically, this means that if you multiply two measurements to obtain, for example, an area from the measured lengths of the sides of a rectangle, the area will have a percentage uncertainty equal to the percentage uncertainty of the least precise side. Suppose that both sides were several hundred feet long measured to the nearest foot (each number having 3 digits). When the product is calculated it would generate 5 or 6 digits. The rule applied here means that only 3 digits of the product are meaningful. Thus 192 × 643 = 123000 or 1.23×10^5, not 123456. Although this rule should be strictly adhered to in all other calculations, it must not be used in least squares calculations. The theoretical reason for this is that in a least squares calculation the data is assumed to be infinitely precise. The practical reason can be more readily seen in the solutions of equations for A and B in the straight-line equation. Both the numerators and denominator of these terms are the difference between products which will turn out to be a small difference between two large numbers of nearly equal magnitude. If these products were to be rounded according to the rule just given, the differences would become meaningless, as would the calculated coefficients. For this reason, all X, Y, and Z quantities in the BASIC program have been defined as double precision numbers (see line 10 in Listing 5-2).

Comparison of Results

The four remaining routines in this program are Options 6-9 and are given in Listing 5-5. The first three are relatively simple service routines that operate on the coefficients obtained from the curve-fitting routines. The fourth routine, Option No. 9, is a short routine which prints the most recent time counts of the eight thermometer elements each time the "T" key is pressed. Since the routine is reading the BUF table that is updated on the quarter minute, you can only get new data printed every 15 seconds. This routine is useful prior to running the calibration experiment to verify that the monostable circuits are functioning properly. It is also useful for observing the fluctuations in count time of the elements while they are nominally at constant temperature. This will give you some idea of the stability of the monostable circuits as well as the randomness (noise) associated with the readings. Additionally, a measure of the response time of the elements to abrupt temperature change can be obtained by touching an element at ambient temperature. The initial temperature rise (decrease in count time) as well as the time to return can be examined in this manner. A return to the Option List from this routine is made by pressing the "Q" key. When the count times are printed to the video screen, their two-byte values are converted to one decimal number and printed in increasing element number order from left to right in one line on the screen.

Option No. 6 is useful for creating a video display of the comparison of a set of experimental calibration data with the calculated results based on the coefficients obtained from a least squares fit. The routine branches depending on whether the least squares fit was for a straight-line or parabolic equation. The printed table is similar to those given in Tables 5-2 and 5-3 with the exception that the temperature residuals and the RMS T are

```
6000 INPUT "THERM.#,A,B,C (IF LINEAR C=0)";K,C3,C2,C1
6010 CLS: IF C1=0 THEN 6100
6020 FOR I=1 TO 15: T=T(I)+459.7
6030 TC=EXP((C3/T+4)+(C2/T+2)+C1)
6040 CO=C1-LOG(CT(I,K))
6050 X=SQR(1/((-C2+SQR(C2+2-(4*C3*CO)))/(2*C3)))-459.7
6060 PRINT T(I),CT(I,K),INT(TC),INT(100*X+0.5)/100,;
6070 NEXT I
6080 PRINT "T(OBS)","CT(OBS)","CT(CALC)","T(CALC)";
6090 A$=INKEY$: IF A$="" THEN 6090 ELSE 100
6100 FOR I=1 TO 15: T=T(I)+459.7
6110 TC=EXP(C3/T+C2)
6120 X=(C3/(LOG(CT(I,K))-C2))-459.7
6130 GOTO 6060
7000 CLS: PRINT "ENTER '999' TO QUIT"
7010 INPUT "A,B,C (IF LINEAR, C=0)";C3,C2,C1
7020 INPUT "COUNT";CT
7030 IF CT=999 THEN 100
7040 IF C1=0 GOTO 7100
7050 CO=C1-LOG(CT)
7060 X=SQR(1/((-C2+SQR(C2+2-(4*C3*CO)))/(2*C3)))-459.7
7070 PRINT "T(F)"INT(100*X+0.5)/100
7080 GOTO 7020
7100 X=(C3/(LOG(CT)-C2))-459.7
7110 GOTO 7070
8000 CLS: PRINT "ENTER '999' TO QUIT"
8010 INPUT "A,B,C (IF LINEAR, C=0)";C3,C2,C1
8020 INPUT "T, DEG.F";T: IF T=999 THEN 100
8030 T=T+459.7
8040 IF C1=0 THEN 8100
8050 TC=EXP((C3/T+4)+(C2/T+2)+C1)
8060 PRINT "COUNT ="INT(TC)
8070 GOTO 8020
8100 TC=EXP(C3/T+C2)
8110 GOTO 8060
9000 CLS: PRINT "PRESS 'T' TO READ THERMOMETER COUNTS, 'Q' TO QUIT"
9010 A$=INKEY$: IF A$="" THEN 9010
9020 IF A$="Q" THEN 100
9030 IF A$<>"T" THEN 9010
9050 FOR I=31888 TO 31910 STEP 3
9060 K=1+LOG(PEEK(I))/LOG(2): X=PEEK(I+1): Y=PEEK(I+2)
9070 CT(1,K)=X+256*Y
9080 PRINT@7*K,CT(1,K);: NEXT I
9090 GOTO 9010
```

Listing 5-5. Thermometer Calibration, Part 3

not calculated. The routine assumes that the data is present in the
CT table—if it is not, the table can be read from the Data
Statements with Option No. 3 prior to executing Option No. 6.

There are basically only two calculations in the routine. One to
convert a temperature to a count time and one to convert a count
time to a temperature. The manner in which either of these
calculations is performed depends, of course, on the form of the
equation. To convert a temperature to a count time for either the
straight-line or parabolic equations requires first converting the
Fahrenheit temperature to absolute by adding 459.7 and then
plugging the absolute temperature into the equation. Since

solving the equation will yield the natural logarithm of the count time, the antilog must be evaluated. The EXP function is the equivalent of taking the natural antilog. Lines 6030 and 6110 perform the operation for the parabolic and straight lines, respectively.

* * * * *

RULE 7. If the parabolic fit is taken versus 1/T instead of (1/T)², change the exponents in lines 6030 and 8050, and delete the first SQR command in line 7060.

* * * * *

To convert a time count to a temperature requires solving the calibration equation for the independent variable. For the straight line, we obtain line 7100 which is a simple rearrangement. For the parabolic equation, we must solve the quadratic equation:

$$Ax^2 + Bx + (C - \log CT) = 0$$

where the quantity in parentheses is a constant (since the value of CT is known). The general solution for a quadratic is:

$$x = \frac{-b \pm \sqrt{b^2 - 4ac}}{2a}$$

where, in the present case, a = A, b = B, and c = (C – log CT). The critical part of the solution is the selection of the + or – sign in front of the square root. Recall that for the parabola (see Fig. 5-1) there are two values of x for each value of y. In line 7060, the plus sign is chosen to yield the values of x (1/T or (1/T)²) lying on the right side of the parabola. Although absurd results are immediately obvious, you should bear in mind that the selection of the sign is the probable cause and check the equation first. Once again we should note that the temperatures used in the equations are absolute and must be converted back to Fahrenheit by subtracting 459.7.

Options No. 7 and No. 8 are just the two calculations performed in Option No. 6: time count to temperature and temperature to time count, respectively. They differ only by allowing input from the keyboard of the quantity to be converted instead of using the calibration values from the CT table. Either option is useful for providing points to plot the smooth "working" curve of count time versus degree F (not the least squares plots of log CT versus 1/T). If, out of curiosity, you decide to plot a working curve, you will most likely find that it will require a graph measuring 15 by 20 inches to see deviations of the experimental points from the calculated curve.

Measurements

The BASIC routines that are convenient for observing the operation of the system are combined into one program called "Time and Temp Summaries." The list of options and the initialization routines that are the first two of these options are provided in Listing 5-6. Lines 10-30 initialize the program and assign four character labels to the seven set-point sensors. These string variables will obviously have to be modified according to your system. There are nine options listed that include three system initialization routines (Options 1, 2, and 9), four display routines (Options 3-6), and two data management routines (Options 7 and 8).

Initialization Routines

Once the calibration coefficients have been obtained for the outdoor thermometer so that the daily high-low temperature data can be saved for ultimate conversion to degree days, the only remaining adjustment to complete the operating monitor system is to select the set-points for the other seven temperature sensors. As we have already seen, it is not necessary to know the actual temperature that these elements sense. All that is required is that they detect when energy (in the form of heat) is being consumed. This is much more easily determined in terms of the time count of the sensors than in terms of temperature because the calibration experiment is avoided. The simplest way to

```
10 CLEAR 500: R$(1)="OILB": R$(2)="RECR": R$(3)="BEDR"
20 R$(4)="LVRM": R$(5)="HOTW": R$(6)="KITC": R$(7)="BATH"
30 DIM T(24)
100 CLS: PRINT: PRINT TAB(12)"TIME AND TEMP SUMMARIES": PRINT
110 PRINT "OPTION #1 - INITIALIZE DATA TABLES"
120 PRINT "OPTION #2 - LOAD SET POINTS INTO DATA TABLE"
130 PRINT "OPTION #3 - DISPLAY 24 HR. HISTOGRAMS"
140 PRINT "OPTION #4 - 24 HR. TIME-ON SCAN"
150 PRINT "OPTION #5 - 24 HR. HI-LO AND CURRENT TEMP. SCAN"
160 PRINT "OPTION #6 - 32 DAY SUMMARY"
170 PRINT "OPTION #7 - RECORD DATA"
180 PRINT "OPTION #8 - READ/WRITE TO DATA TABLES"
190 PRINT "OPTION #9 - AUTO LOAD OF SET POINTS"
200 PRINT: PRINT TAB(12)"";: INPUT "SELECT OPTION #";A
210 IF A>9 THEN 200
220 ON A GOTO 1000,2000,3000,4000,5000,6000,7000,8000,9000
230 GOTO 200
1000 X=32192: REM S.A. 32 DAY DATA = 7DC0(HEX)
1010 FOR I=0 TO 31: FOR J=0 TO 17
1020 POKE X+18*I+J,I: NEXT J: NEXT I
1100 X=32096: REM S.A. 24 HI/LO TEMP = 7D60(HEX)
1110 FOR I=X TO X+92 STEP 4
1120 POKE I,152: POKE I+1,8: POKE I+2,15: POKE I+3,39
1130 NEXT I
1200 X=31912: REM S.A. 24 HR. TIME-ON SUMS = 7CA8(HEX)
1210 FOR I=0 TO 6: FOR J=2 TO 25
1220 POKE X+I*26+J,0: NEXT J: NEXT I
1230 GOTO 100
2000 INPUT "THERMOMETER # (0 TO QUIT)";N
2010 IF N=0 THEN 100
2020 INPUT "SET POINT COUNT VALUE";CN
2030 I=7-N: H=INT(CN/256): L=CN-256*H
2040 POKE 31912+I*26,L: POKE 31913+I*26,H
2050 GOTO 2000
```

Listing 5-6. Time and Temp Summaries, Part 1

proceed is to first attach the elements to surfaces that respond
(get hot) to the particular energy "drains" you wish to monitor.
Of the seven QDTs in the author's home monitoring system,
three are attached to the separate zone supply pipes of an oil-fired
hot water heating system, one is attached to the flue surface of
the oil burner, one is attached to the domestic hot water supply
from the coil in the oil furnace, and the remaining two are
attached to the hot water supply lines to the kitchen and baths,
respectively. Electrical vinyl tape was used to attach the six
elements connecting to hot water pipes. The element attached to
the galvanized flue pipe was wedged under a small piece of sheet
metal that was fastened to the flue pipe with a sheet metal screw.
Once the elements have been positioned, the monitor program
can be started.

Option No. 1 of the program initializes the three data tables:
BASE, DAY, and MONTH. MONTH which is the monthly

operating summary consisting of 32 days of nine two-byte locations (18 bytes) per day is filled consecutively with integers from 0 to 31. Each low byte of the same day has the same value (each high byte is zero) corresponding to the day number. There is no significance to this pattern other than convenience for one of the display routines. The BASE table that stores the 24 hourly time-on counts for the 7 set-point thermometers (and also the set-point values of each device) is initialized to all zeros. The CTEMP and DAY tables store the most recent time count of the outdoor thermometer in the first 2 bytes of the table followed by the 24 hourly low and high thermometer time counts where each time count also uses two bytes. These values are converted to degrees Fahrenheit in a subroutine that takes the logarithm of the value (see below). Negative values (high byte of the count greater than 127) will cause the subroutine to abort the program with an FC error. For this reason and also because the monitor routine can only replace the current hour low temperature with a time count which corresponds to a lower temperature (similarly for the high temperature), the initialization routine loads the four bytes of each hour with specific values. The values listed in line 1120 set the low temperature at 95° and the high temperature at 5° for the particular QDT used in the author's system. You can change these values to suit yourself, although they will probably work satisfactorily. The only wrinkle may be if the 95° value on your QDT would generate a temperature greater than 99 because 3 digits will crowd the display in one of the routines.

Option No. 2 is used to assign set-point values individually to the seven sensors. The procedure to select a set-point value is most easily accomplished by trial and error. Using one of the display options (see the following section), the time-on counts, set-point values, and current time count for each sensor over the 24-hour period can be continuously observed. By noting the current time count when each of the energy drains is activated, the set point for that sensor can be adjusted using Option No. 2. Because there will be a response lag between the actual drain and the sensor, both when the drain turns on and when it turns off, the set point should be readjusted to a value that measures an equal time duration. Fig. 5-2 illustrates this situation, although it is probably not necessary actually to make a plot in order to

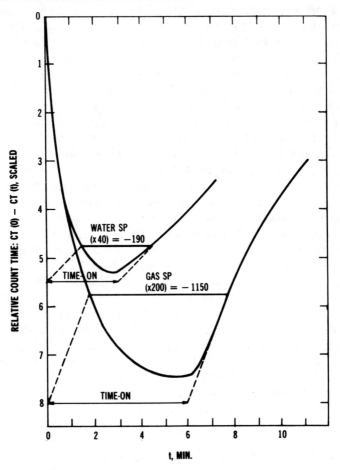

Figure 5-2
QDT response curves for hot water and flue gas.

determine the desired setting of the set point. Once each of the devices has been adjusted, you have completed the system initialization.

Display Routines

Options 3 through 6 are routines that display various portions of the data stored in memory. These routines are presented in Listing 5-7. Because the hourly data is retained only for 24 hours,

```
3000 CLS: FOR R=0 TO 24 STEP 24: FOR C=7 TO 103 STEP 32
3010 FOR Y=0 TO R+18 STEP 2: SET (C,Y): NEXT Y
3020 FOR X=C TO C+24 STEP 2: SET (X,R+18): NEXT X
3030 NEXT C: NEXT R
3040 PRINT@451,"OUT TEMP"TAB(19)R$(7)TAB(35)R$(6)TAB(51)R$(5);
3050 PRINT@963,R$(4)TAB(19)R$(3)TAB(35)R$(2)TAB(51)R$(1);
3060 FOR J=0TO1: FOR I=0TO3: OX=8+32*I: OY=18+24*J
3070 IF J+I>0 THEN 3140
3080 FOR H=0TO23: X=H+8: T=256*PEEK(32096+4*H+1)+PEEK(32096+4*H)
3090 GOSUB 3200: T(H)=(65-T)/5: IF T>65 THEN 3110
3100 FOR Y=T(H) TO 0 STEP -1: SET (X,Y): NEXT Y: GOTO 3130
3110 T=256*PEEK(32098+4*H+1)+PEEK(32098+4*H): GOSUB 3200
3120 T(H)=18-(T-65)/5: FOR Y=T(H)TO18: SET (X,Y): NEXT Y
3130 NEXT H: GOTO 3180
3140 FOR H=0TO23: T(H)=PEEK(31912+26*(4*J+I-1)+H+2)/4: NEXT H
3150 FOR H=0TO23: P=INT(T(H)/4): X=OX+H: IF T(H)=0 THEN 3170
3160 FOR Y=OY-P-1 TO OY-1: SET (X,Y): NEXT Y
3170 NEXT H
3180 NEXT I: NEXT J
3190 A$=INKEY$: IF A$="" THEN 3190 ELSE 100
3200 A=2.08925E11: B=-568953: CC=7.36135
3210 C=CC-LOG(T)
3220 T=(-B+SQR(B↑2-(4*A*C)))/(2*A)
3230 T=SQR(1/T)-459.7: RETURN
4000 B$="####": CLS: FOR I=0 TO 11: IF I=0 THEN H=12 ELSE H=I
4010 PRINT@4*I+7,"";: PRINTUSINGB$;H;: NEXT I
4020 PRINT TAB(58)":"TAB(61)":";
4030 FOR J=7 TO 1 STEP -1: PRINT@((8-J)*128-64),R$(J);
4040 PRINT TAB(5)"AM"TAB(57)"CT=": PRINT " #"J"PM"TAB(57)"SP=";: NEXT J
4050 M=31912: FOR I=0 TO 6: X=PEEK(M+26*I): Y=PEEK(M+26*I)
4060 C=X+256*Y: PRINT@188+128*I,"";: PRINTUSINGB$;C;: NEXT I
4070 PRINT@71,"";: M=31914: FOR I=0 TO 6: FOR K=0 TO 1
4080 FOR J=0 TO 11: PRINTUSINGB$;PEEK(M+26*I+12*K+J);: NEXT J
4090 PRINT@135+I*128+K*64,"";: NEXT K: NEXT I
4100 M=31888: FOR J=1 TO 8: I=0
4110 IF I.21 THEN J=8: GOTO 4150
4120 IF 2↑J AND PEEK(M+I)<>2↑J THEN I=I+3: GOTO 4110
4130 X=PEEK(M+I+1): Y=PEEK(M+I+2): PRINT@128*(8-J)-4,"";
4140 C=X+256*Y: PRINTUSINGB$;C;
4150 NEXT J: FOR L=0 TO 600
4160 A$=INKEY$: IF A$<>"" THEN 100
4170 NEXT L: GOSUB 9100: GOTO 4050
5000 CLS: B$="###": PRINT@0,"";
5010 T=PEEK(32094)+256*PEEK(32095): GOSUB 3200: PRINTUSINGB$;T
5020 FOR J=0 TO 23: I=32096+4*J: IF J<10 PRINT " ";
5030 PRINT J";";: T=PEEK(I)+256*PEEK(I+1): GOSUB 3200
5040 PRINTUSINGB$;T;: PRINT "/";
5050 T=PEEK(I+2)+256*PEEK(I+3): GOSUB 3200
5060 PRINTUSINGB$;T;: PRINT,;: NEXT J
5070 FOR J=0TO1400: A$=INKEY$: IF A$<>"" THEN 100
5080 NEXT J: PRINT@0,"";: GOSUB 9100: GOTO 5010
6000 B$="####": X=32192: FOR I=0 TO 31
6010 PRINT I+1" DAYS PREVIOUS": FOR J=0 TO 17
6020 PRINTUSINGB$; PEEK(X+18*I+J);
6030 NEXT J: PRINT
6040 A$=INKEY$: IF A$="" THEN 6040
6050 NEXT I: GOTO 100
```

Listing 5-7. Time and Temp Summaries, Part 2

after which it is totaled and saved as daily sums, the first three of these routines display the data obtained during the past 24 hours. There is not much that is new to these routines that we have not already considered. Formatting of the display data follows standard Level II BASIC programming techniques. It should be noted that all three routines call the subroutine, beginning at line 3200, which converts the count time of the outdoor thermometer to degrees.

RULE 8. Revise line 3200 to equate to the calibration
coefficients of the outdoor thermometer.

* * * * *

Return from these three routines to the Option List is made by
pressing any key.

A sample display of the histograms produced by Option No. 3 is
shown in Fig. 5-3. Since the results of all eight elements are
displayed on the screen, the titling has been kept to a minimum to
reduce the appearance of clutter. The OUT TEMP graph in the
upper left corner gives the results of the temperature in
Fahrenheit degrees spanning 5° per vertical interval. To permit
easy conversion, only alternate blocks (pixels) are displayed on the
axes. The horizontal axis for this and the other seven graphs are
clock hours ranging from midnight (0 hour) to 11 PM (23 hour): the

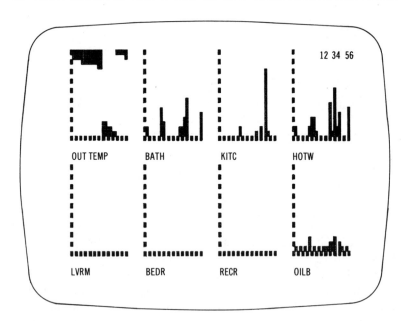

Figure 5-3
Histogram display.

odd numbered hours being marked with pixels. To extend the temperature range in the OUT TEMP graph, both the top and bottom edges of the graph correspond to 65°F. Bars extending downward represent the hourly low temperature whenever the low temperature is below 65 with the topmost pixel corresponding to 60-64, the second interval to 55-59, etc. When the hourly low temperature is 65°F or above, then the hourly high temperature is plotted up from the bottom of the graph where the lowest interval corresponds to 65-69, the next to 70-75, etc. This technique provides a double range of −25 to 65 for the hourly low temperature and 65 to 154(!) for the hourly high temperature.

The reason for folding the temperature at 65, besides allowing an adequate range of reasonable detail, is related to the heating (and cooling) loads on the house. Roughly, the area at the top of the graph minus the area at the bottom is proportional to the number of (heating) degree days for the past 24 hours. Similarly, the reverse difference in summer approximates the number of "cooling" degree days.

One other aspect of this graph, as well as the other seven, is to note that the horizontal axis plots the time as clock hours from left to right. Thus, since in this example the current time (displayed in the upper right corner of the screen) is the noon hour, the left half of each graph shows the data of the morning of the present day while the right half of each graph displays the data of the previous afternoon and night. The particular data represented in Fig. 5-3. was taken from a day in mid-April to emphasize this point. The previous day had been warm when a cold front moved through the area during the night. Typically, the coldest time of day occurs during the hour preceding sunrise.

Fig. 5-4 shows the tabular display of the data for the set-point elements obtained with Option No. 4. This is the display referred to previously in the description of adjusting the set-point values. In order to fit all the data onto the screen, the 24 hours are printed onto 2 rows of AM and PM for each of the set-point sensors. Each sensor is labeled and numbered in the left-hand column with its current count time and the set-point value given in the far right-hand column. The contents of the table are the total time-on per hour given in quarter-minutes. The data in this table are the same

	12	1	2	3	4	5	6	7	8	9	10	11	12:34:56
BATH AM	25						83	45					CT=3117
# 7 PM			28	20	47	129						69	SP=2700
KITC AM									31				CT=3859
# 6 PM				16		22		209	5				SP=3250
HOTW AM	24						21	61	64	13			CT=3073
# 5 PM				103	9	146	31	76				94	SP=2400
LVRM AM													CT=3094
# 4 PM													SP=2000
BEDR AM													CT=3452
# 3 PM													SP=2000
RECR AM													CT=3623
# 2 PM													SP=2000
OILB AM	10		10		11		45		15		9		CT=1234
# 1 PM	4		13	30	24	45		37	7		9		SP=1400

Figure 5-4
Time-on display.

that was plotted in Fig. 5-3. Note that the bar height in the histogram is the integer (rounded up) of the data value divided by 16 (number of quarter-minutes per 4-minute interval).

This table and the table of low/high hourly outdoor temperatures from Option No. 5 are updated approximately every 15 seconds. The corresponding programmed wait loops are in lines 4150 and 5050, respectively. The display obtained with Option No. 5 is shown in Fig 5-5. The current temperature is printed in the upper left corner of the screen.

Option No. 6 lists the 32 daily summaries of the set-point sensors and the low and high temperature. A maximum of five consecutive days can be viewed on the screen at one time as shown in Fig. 5-6. The data is advanced by one day with each key press.

Since this is a memory dump, the raw data is presented; that is, the decimal values of the individual memory bytes are listed in the order: low byte, high byte proceeding from device No. 7 to device No. 0. The four bytes for device No. 0 (outdoor thermometer) list

```
50                                              12 34 56

  0 : 56/ 59      1 : 56/ 58      2 : 56/ 58      3 : 56/ 57

  4 : 54/ 57      5 : 53/ 56      6 : 54/ 56      7 : 54/ 56

  8 : 51/ 55      9 : 51/ 53     10 : 50/ 53     11 : 48/ 52

 12 : 49/ 51     13 : 71/ 75     14 : 72/ 76     15 : 71/ 75

 16 : 71/ 73     17 : 68/ 71     18 : 65/ 69     19 : 64/ 65

 20 : 62/ 64     21 : 62/ 63     22 : 61/ 62     23 : 57/ 62
```

Figure 5-5
Low/high temperature display.

the low temperature bytes before the high temperature bytes.
Since each pair of bytes corresponds to base 256 arithmetic, the
value of each count may be calculated as (low byte) + 256*(high
byte). The utility of this routine is to allow one to make a backup
copy of the raw data during periods that power failure could ruin
critical data. The only way to exit this routine and return to the
Option List (other than a BREAK and RUN) is to advance through
all 32 days.

Data Management Routines

A more compact summary of the monthly data is available by
selecting Option No. 7. Although its principal function is to store
the data on cassette tape, the routine can be run without turning
on the tape recorder. The program routine is given in Listing 5-8
and a sample display is shown in Fig. 5-7. Note that the
subroutine at line 3200 is also called from this routine. Refined
data is displayed (and recorded); that is, the two-byte time-on
counts are converted to single decimal values and the temperature
count times are converted to Fahrenheit degrees.

The data is grouped into blocks of five days with a last block
containing the excess of the five-day multiple. Each block is
written as a single string variable with the data values separated
by single spaces and the first entry being the date of the first day

```
1 DAYS PREVIOUS

244   1 253   0 174   2   0   0   0   0   0   0  24   1 193  13

178  10

2 DAYS PREVIOUS

 57   1  42   1 120   3   0   0   0   0   0   0 230   0  99  15

122  10

3 DAYS PREVIOUS

213   0 186   0  54   2  13   1   0   0   0   0   5   1 156  16

206  11

4 DAYS PREVIOUS

 96   1 211   1 212   2   0   0   0   0   0   0   8   1 254  14

 13  13

5 DAYS PREVIOUS

123   1   4   1  39   2  82   5   0   0   0   0 172   1  32  20

101  11
```

Figure 5-6 ————————————————————————————————————
Monthly summary display.

in the block. Dates are computed in the routine based on the current day's date. Months of 28, 29 (leap year), 30, and 31 days are determined in the subroutine at line 7300. Even with a few counts of blank tape inserted between separate recordings, a year's data will easily fit on one side (30 min.) of a 60-minute cassette.

When actually recording data, a BREAK must be executed and the clock stopped by pressing the Reset button: do NOT overlook Rules 2 and 3. After the recording is completed, the clock should be resumed with Rule 1.

The last two routines in the program are given in Listing 5-9. Option No. 8 is for rebuilding any entry or set of entries in any of the data tables in memory excepting the set-point values. Option

```
        SELECT OPTION #? 7

LAST DAY SAVED (M#,D#,Y#)? 4,3,81

TODAY'S DATE (M#,D#,Y#)? 4,13,81

SAVING 1 5-DAY BLOCKS

AND 1 4-DAY BLOCK

 40481 396 210 543 0 0 0 216 59 72 480 243 755 0 0 0 216 41 62 3

07 203 709 1587 0 0 440 31 50 292 228 587 2393 0 528 569 24 60 3

79 260 551 1362 0 0 428 34 71

CLOCK OFF! - READY CASSETTE - HIT ENTER?

 40981 352 467 724 0 0 0 264 51 60 213 186 566 269 0 0 261 45 68

 313 298 888 0 0 0 230 49 78 498 253 686 0 0 0 280 57 76

CLOCK OFF! - READY CASSETTE - HIT ENTER? _
```

Listing 5-8. Time and Temp Summaries, Part 3

```
7000 INPUT "LAST DAY SAVED (M#,D#,Y#)";ML,DL,YL
7010 INPUT "TODAY'S DATE (M#,D#,Y#)";MC,DC,YC
7020 MD=0: IF MC=ML GOTO 7050
7030 IF MC-ML>1 THEN ND=32: B=6: RD=2: GOSUB 7300: GOTO 7060
7040 GOSUB 7300
7050 ND=DC+MD-DL-1: B=INT(ND/5): RD=ND-5*B
7060 PRINT "SAVING"B"5-DAY BLOCKS"
7070 IF RD>0 THEN PRINT "AND 1"STR$(RD)"-DAY BLOCK"
7080 YR=YL: MR=ML: DR=DL-4
7090 FOR I=ND-5 TO -4 STEP -5: DR=DR+5
7100 IF MR<>MC AND DR>MD THEN DR=DR-MD: MR=MR+1: IF MR<>MC THEN ML=ML+1: GOSUB 7300
7110 IF MR=13 THEN MR=1: YR=YR+1
7120 D$=STR$(MR*10↑4+DR*10↑2+YR)
7130 FOR J=4 TO 0 STEP -1: IF I+J<0 GOTO 7180
7140 FOR K=0 TO 8: M=32192+18*(I+J)+2*K
7150 T=PEEK(M)+256*PEEK(M+1)
7160 IF K=>7 GOSUB 3200
7170 D$=D$+STR$(INT(0.5+T)): NEXT K
7180 NEXT J
7190 PRINT D$: INPUT "CLOCK OFF! - READY CASSETTE - HIT ENTER";Q
7200 PRINT#-1,D$: NEXT I: GOTO 100
7300 ON ML GOTO 7340,7310,7340,7330,7340,7330,7340,7340,7330,7340,7330,7340
7310 IF YL/4=INT(YL/4) THEN MD=29 ELSE MD=28
7320 RETURN
7330 MD=30: RETURN
7340 MD=31: RETURN
```

Figure 5-7
Cassette record display.

```
8000 CLS: PRINT: PRINT "DATA TABLE  1ST ADDRESS  FORMAT       DESCRIPTION"
8010 PRINT: PRINT "#1  BUF        31888     8 X (1S+1D)  RECENT DEV. CODE + COUNT"
8020 PRINT "#2  BASE       31912     7 X (1D+24S)  SET PT. + HOURLY TIME-ON"
8030 PRINT "#3  CTEMP      32094     1 X 1D     CURRENT TEMP. COUNT"
8040 PRINT "#4  TEMP       32096    24 X 2D     HOURLY LO/HI THERM. COUNTS"""
8050 PRINT "#5  MTOP       32192    32 X (7D+2D)  DAILY TIME-ON/DEV. + LO/HI T"
8060 INPUT "SELECT TABLE (0 TO QUIT)";A
8070 ON A GOTO 8100,8200,8300,8400,8500
8080 GOTO 100
8100 PRINT "BUF TABLE UPDATED EVERY 15 SECONDS: 8 X (1S+1D)"
8110 FOR I=31888TO31911STEP3: PRINT LOG(PEEK(I))/LOG(2),PEEK(I+1)+256*PEEK(I+2): NEXT I
8120 PRINT: PRINT "PRESS ANY KEY TO RESUME"
8130 A$=INKEY$: IF A$="" THEN 8130 ELSE 8000
8200 PRINT "TO CHANGE SET POINT USE OPTION LIST #2"
8210 PRINT "ENTER NEW VALUE OR RE-ENTER OLD VALUE"
8220 PRINT "ENTER '0,0' TO QUIT"
8230 INPUT "SELECT DEVICE (1-7) AND HOUR (0-23)";I,J
8240 IF I=0 GOTO 8000
8250 M=31912+(7-I)*26+2+J: PRINT M,PEEK(M)
8260 INPUT X: POKE M,X
8270 GOTO 8200
8300 PRINT "LO BYTE","HI BYTE","DEGS. F"
8310 X=PEEK(32094): Y=PEEK(32095): T=X+256*Y
8320 GOSUB 3200: PRINT X,Y,T
8330 PRINT "PRESS ANY KEY TO RESUME"
8340 A$=INKEY$: IF A$="" THEN 8340 ELSE 8000
8400 PRINT "DATA FOR EACH HOUR - LSB LO, MSB LO, LSB HI, MSB HI"
8410 PRINT "                    LO T DEGREES    HI T DEGREES"
8420 INPUT "SELECT HOUR (0-23) (24 TO QUIT)";I
8430 IF I>23 GOTO 8000
8440 M=32096+4*I: PRINT PEEK(M),PEEK(M+1),PEEK(M+2),PEEK(M+3)
8450 T=PEEK(M)+256*(PEEK(M+1)): GOSUB 3200: PRINT T;
8460 T=PEEK(M+2)+256*(PEEK(M+3)): GOSUB 3200: PRINT ,;T
8470 INPUT "ENTER 4 BYTES IN ORDER";N1,N2,N3,N4
8480 POKE M,N1: POKE M+1,N2: POKE M+2,N3: POKE M+3,N4
8490 GOTO 8400
8500 PRINT "DEV.#","ADDRESS=LO BYTE","ADDRESS=HI BYTE","PRODUCT"
8510 INPUT "ENTER PREVIOUS DAY (1-32)";I
8520 M=32192+18*(I-1): FOR J=0TO6: GOSUB 8590: NEXT J
8530 PRINT "#"7-J,M+2*J"="X,M+1+2*J"="Y,X+256*Y: NEXT J
8540 J=7: GOSUB 8590: PRINT "LO T",M+2*J"="X,M+1+2*J"="Y,X+256*Y
8550 J=8: GOSUB 8590: PRINT "HI T",M+2*J"="X,M+1+2*J"="Y,X+256*Y
8560 INPUT "ENTER ADDRESS,BYTE TO CHANGE (0,0 TO QUIT)";X,Y
8570 IF T=0 GOTO 8000
8580 POKE T,Y: GOTO 8560
8590 X=PEEK(M+2*J): Y=PEEK(M+1+2*J): RETURN
9000 FOR I=1 TO 7: READ CN
9010 H=INT(CN/256): L=CN-256*H
9020 POKE 31912+(7-I)*26,L: POKE 31913+(7-I)*26,H
9030 NEXT I
9040 RESTORE: GOTO 100
9050 DATA 1400,2000,2000,2000,2400,3250,2700
9100 FOR I=1 TO 7: READ CN
9110 H=INT(CN/256): L=CN-256*H: M=31912+(7-I)*26
9120 IF PEEK(M)<>L THEN POKE M,L
9130 IF PEEK(M+1)<>H THEN POKE M+1,H
9140 NEXT I
9150 RESTORE: RETURN
```

Listing 5-9. Time and Temp Summaries, Part 4

No. 9 uses the only data statement in the program to rewrite all set-point values in one operation. The only real need for either of these routines is in the instance of a crash due to power failure (assuming you have kept a backup copy of the raw data from Option No. 6) or in those rare cases when a power flicker (surge) may scramble a few memory locations. This has happened in the author's system just often enough to make these routines worthwhile to be on-line. On a few occasions the clock will still be running at the correct time, the monitor program will be properly loaded, and yet a set-point value will hold garbage. In a suspenders-and-belt attempt to avoid bad data due to a muffed set point, a final subroutine is added beginning at line 9100 that uses the data statement set points to check that these values are correct. This subroutine is executed during the wait loops of Options 4 and 5.

One final note: if you are faced with ruined data and need to delete one or more days in the monthly summary (MONTH), it is probably best to zero all time-on counts and insert the low and high bytes of both the daily low and high temperatures with values that will convert to 65° (see Option No. 8 of the Calibration Program). If the temperature values were zeroed, the program would abort when it attempted to take the log of zero. This will preserve the date order and not invalidate future calculations on the rest of the data.

Summary

Three BASIC language service programs have been listed and described. Some aspects of the descriptions include:
1. A machine language load of the TNT Monitor with checksum error detection.
2. Eight rules to be observed in running the system.
3. Details for calibrating either a thermistor or quad-diode thermometer using apparatus (mostly) available in the home.
4. Two least squares curve-fitting routines covering both straight-line and parabolic curves and some of the pitfalls of curve fitting.
5. Several routines for system initialization, observation, and data management.

Estimating Home Heat Loss

Chapter 6————————————————————

The collection of data is the first step in energy management. When you have operated your system long enough to acquire a data base, you are in a position to consider various options to improve your energy economy. In the meantime, there is the possibility of estimating the "theoretical" heat loss from a home. This estimate can serve as a guide to what you can expect under ideal (textbook) conditions in terms of actual (or absolute) heat loss. More importantly, it can serve in relative terms by letting you compare the effect of altered conditions as a percentage change of the ideal.

A computer program to calculate the heat loss from a residence is presented in Appendix C. This is a fairly complicated program that computes the total loss of heat (measured in BTU) in one hour for each Fahrenheit degree difference between the inside and outside temperatures. We shall not detail all the calculations and assumptions involved although these can be deduced by anyone with a sufficient engineering background by working through the program. We shall outline the broad method of the program so the interested individual can follow the procedures involved.

Essentially, heat flow is analogous to electrical current (charge flow) and is governed by Fourier's law in the identical manner to Ohm's law for electricity. We present this analogy on the assumption that readers interested in computer interfacing are likely to be more familiar with electronics than thermodynamics. Table 6-1 compares the important quantities. One significant

Table 6-1. Analogy Between Heat and Electricity

	Electronics	Thermodynamics
1. Quantity transported	Q, coulomb	q, BTU*
2. Rate of transport	I, ampere = coulomb/sec	J, BTU/(sq.ft.)(hr)
3. Potential	V, voltage	T, temperature
4. Driving force	E, volts	dT, degrees
5. Conductance	1/R, amp/volt	U, BTU/(sq.ft.)(hr)(deg)
6. Resistance	R, ohm	R = 1/U
7. Law	Ohm: I = E/R	Fourier: J = U dT

*BTU (British Thermal Unit): the amount of heat required to raise the temperature of 1 lb. of water by 1 °F.

difference is the way the cross sectional area of the conductor is treated. In working with heat flow, the area is explicitly expressed, whereas in the electrical case, it is implicitly carried in the resistance term. A second distinction is that in heat flow the property of interest is conductance, rather than resistance, as in the electrical case.

In calculating heat loss, we wish to know the number of BTUs that escape from the building to the outside, or equivalently, how many BTUs must be added (by burning fuel) in order to balance those lost. Based on Fourier's law, the number of BTUs, q, we need to calculate are given by the equation:

$$q = (U \times A) \times dT \times t$$

where,
A is the number of square feet (surface area) having a conductance U,
dT is the difference between the inside and outside temperatures,
t is the period of time.

It is apparent that the different surface areas of walls, windows and doors, floors, and ceilings will have different conductances depending on the materials of construction. In this respect, the conductances of adjacent surface areas are additive. However, in calculating the conductance of a given area consisting of layers of materials, such as a wall consisting of a layer of plaster, insulation and studs, sheathing, and siding, it is the resistances of the layers that are additive. The total conductance is then obtained as the reciprocal of the total resistance for that area. The electrical analogy is the resistor network shown in Fig. 6-1.

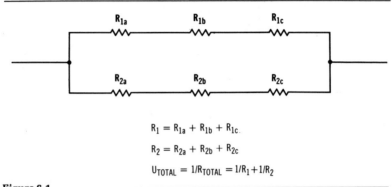

$$R_1 = R_{1a} + R_{1b} + R_{1c}$$
$$R_2 = R_{2a} + R_{2b} + R_{2c}$$
$$U_{TOTAL} = 1/R_{TOTAL} = 1/R_1 + 1/R_2$$

Figure 6-1
Resistor analogy of heat loss.

Method of Calculation

In order to sort out areas of different conductances, the computer program divides the calculation into a set of nested loops by first dividing the house into a number of rooms or other heated spaces, then subdividing each room into a maximum of up to four areas. For each room area, each outside (exposed) wall is calculated with each wall opening (windows and doors) treated separately, followed by the ceiling and floor for the room area. The total heat loss for the house is obtained by summing the individual net heat losses for each room. The net heat loss for each room is the sum of the heat losses calculated for walls (partitions), windows and doors, ceiling, floor, and a final term called infiltration. The infiltration term evaluates the heat lost due to exchange of air in the room with outside air.

The overall organization of the program uses lines 100-120 for initialization, lines 125-670 for the actual calculations using the nested loops, lines 690-960 for summary listings including related subroutines, lines 970-990 for data statements, and lines 1000-2003 for calculation subroutines. The nested loops and their associated indices span the following program segments:

Line 140 I = ROOM NUMBER,
160 J = AREA NUMBER,
210 K = PARTITION NUMBER,
325 L = WINDOW NUMBER,
430 NEXT L,
455 NEXT K,
670 NEXT J: NEXT I.

Dimensioned variables used in the calculations are listed in Table 6-2.

Table 6–2. Program Dimensioned Variables

NUMBER OF DATA:	Q(7)	Insulation resistance
	R(12)	Construction resistance
	U(6,3)	Window/door conductance
NUMBER OF ROOMS:	RM$(NR)	Room name
	LT(NR)	Total heat loss
	LI(NR)	Infiltration heat loss
	LP(NR)	Partition heat loss
	LW(NR)	Window/door heat loss
	LC(NR)	Ceiling heat loss
	LF(NR)	Floor heat loss
MAXIMUM AREAS:	CC(4)	Ceiling code
	FC(4)	Floor code
	RW(4)	Area width
	RL(4)	Area length
	NP(4)	Number of exposed partitions
AREA, WALL:	PA(4,4)	Net partition surface area/wall
	PL(4,4)	Partition length
	PH(4,4)	Partition height
	PD$(4,4)	Partition direction
	PC(4,4)	Partition construction code— Resistance/unit area
	PU(4,4)	Partition conductance/unit area
	NW(4,4)	Number of windows and doors
	WA(4,4)	Total window area (square feet)
	WS(4,4)	Total window conductance

The program uses the video display to prompt the user for the necessary information (consisting mostly of dimensions and codes). The upper part of the screen lists the current room, area number, and input requests. The lower portion of the screen alternately displays various lists from which the user selects code numbers for types of construction and insulation. The seven lists used in coding are shown in Table 6-3.

Table 6–3. Construction and Insulation Code Lists

Wall Construction:	1 = WOODFRAME, SIDING	2 = WOODFRAME, UNSHEATHED
	3 = MASONRY, FURRED	4 = MASONRY, PLAIN
	5 = BELOW GRADE (18'')	
Fiber Insulation:	1 = BLANKET/BATT	2 = LOOSE/BLOWN
Expanded Types:	3 = URETHANE 4 = RUBBER	5 = STYRENE/OTHER
Special Types:	6 = ROOF DECK SLAB	7 = FLOOR PERIMETER SLAB
Type:	1 = CASED WINDOW (0.75 CFM)	2 = CASED WINDOW
	3 = FIXED/PICTURE	4 = JALOUSIE
	5 = SLIDING GLASS DOORS	6 = OTHER DOOR
Class:	1 = SINGLE GLASS	
	2 = DOUBLE GLASS	
	3 = STORM SASH	
Insulation:	1 = NONE	
	2 = WEATHER STRIPPING OR STORM DOOR (NOT BOTH)	
	3 = BOTH WEATHER STRIPPING AND STORM DOOR	
Floor Type:	1 = OVER CLOSED SPACE	2 = OVER VENTED SPACE/ GARAGE
	3 = ON GRADE SLAB	4 = BELOW GRADE SLAB (>18'')
Ceiling Type:	1 = UNDER VENTED ROOF/SPACE	
	2 = EXPOSED BEAMS OR RAFTERS	
	3 = COMBINED ROOF-CEILING	

The ultimate validity of the calculations rests both on the detail of the calculations and on the conductance and resistance values employed. As can be seen from Table 6-3, this program uses a rather small data base suitable for conventional construction. There are extensive engineering data tables, most of which can be traced to the American Society of Heating, Refrigeration, and Air Conditioning Engineers (ASHRAE). In particular, the *ASHRAE Handbook of Fundamentals (1972 edition)* provides extensive tables and methods of calculation. In addition, two secondary sources that provide simplified tables and methods are *Guide H-21 (1968)* of The Institute of Boiler and Radiator Manufacturers (I B R) and *Manual J (3rd edition, 1967)* of the National Warm Air Heating and Air Conditioning Association. All three sources were used to prepare the data base used in this program. The algorithm used in this program and the estimates made do not reflect the precision of the engineering data base. In most cases, smoothing approximations were made by the author. Without any other guide than intuition, I would "guesstimate" the accuracy of the calculated results to be within ± 20%.

The data provided in the data statements are assigned in the READ statements to the U table, and the R and Q lists. The U table contains the conductances for various standard windows and doors. The R list stores the resistances for standard thicknesses of walls, floors, and ceilings. The Q list holds the resistance values (per inch thickness) of the more common insulating materials. The data values and their relation to the Code Lists of Table 6-3 are given in Table 6-4.

The only data not already considered is used to calculate the air infiltration loss. The program uses an algorithm based on a modification of the I B R method. This quantity is undoubtedly the most difficult one to make even with good engineering data, given the uncertainties of wind velocities, the vagaries of construction, and the habits of the occupants. This method introduces a loss factor for a room area that depends on the number of outside walls having window or door openings, the room volume, and a factor based on either the wall constructions or the window or door construction. The infiltration loss per room is the sum of the losses of the areas in the room. The equation for the loss per room area is

$$0.009 * AN * (RW * RL * PH) * AF$$

where,
AN is the number of walls with openings,
the quantity in parentheses is the volume of the room area

(width × length × height),
AF is the air factor.

Table 6–4. Data for Conductance and Resistance

U(Type, Class):		Class:	1	2	3
	Type:	1	1.50	0.95	0.90
		2	2.55	2.05	1.20
		3	1.40	0.85	0.85
		4	7.50	7.50	2.20
		5	2.50	2.00	2.00
		6	4.50	2.40	1.30
	Insulation:		1	2	3

R(Code): (/standard thickness)				Q(Code): (/inch thickness)	
1		3.75	**Wall Construction**	1	3.70
2		1.50		2	3.33
3		3.33		3	5.88
4		2.08		4	4.55
5		16.5		5	3.45
6	(1)	7.14	**Floor Type**	6	2.77
7	(2)	3.57		7	0.33
8	(3)	1.33			
9	(4)	33.1			
10	(1)	1.53	**Ceiling Type**		
11	(2)	3.22			
12	(3)	3.22			

The air factor value is assigned according to the criteria: 2.5 for either unsheathed woodframe or plain masonry walls; 2.0 for uninsulated doors or single glass windows; 1.0 for all other areas having exposed walls; and 0 (initialized value) when there are no outside walls. The higher value is taken in cases where more than one criterion is satisfied.

Results of Calculation

Typically, the intent of a heat load calculation is to determine the size of the furnace (boiler) and the required sizes of radiators or air ducts for each room. Based on the equation for q, such calculations have to assume a typical worst case outdoor temperature, a comfortable indoor temperature, and a time period. Because heat output ratings of equipment are usually specified on a per hour basis, the time period is taken as one hour. The usual indoor temperature is taken as 70 or 75°F: even taking conservation into account, in design specifications it is best to allow for some margin of error. The outdoor design temperature is obtained from weather data over a 25-30 year period and corresponds to the temperature which is exceeded only 1-3% of the time during the winter months. The outdoor design temperature obviously depends on geographical location. This program is not meant to be used for design conditions. The value of the calculational data developed here is for comparison under normal operating conditions.

When the calculations are complete, five heat loss values for each room will be assigned. These correspond to the losses through the ceiling, walls, floor, windows and doors, and air (infiltration). Each loss is in units of BTU/(hr)(deg) where the deg term is the difference between the indoor and outdoor temperatures. Nine summary tables are available for listing to the video display. Each table consists of a line for each room and six columns of data corresponding to the five loss values mentioned and their total. One table presents the individual losses as the percentage of the total loss for the house (Option No. 5). The remaining eight tables are divided into two groups. Options 1-4 present the data calculated on the loss per degree day, while Options 6-9 present the data calculated on the loss per hour (for indoor and outdoor temperatures input by the user). Each group of four Options list the data in terms of the four different energy units: BTUs, gallons of fuel oil, standard cubic feet of natural gas, and kilowatt hours of electricity. The conversion factors used to modify the base calculations are given in lines 755-795. The energy conversion factors are attributed to the U.S. Department of Energy figures and were quoted in the national press. There is undoubtedly some uncertainty in the figures due to the various sources of fuel. Where tables exceed the screen size and when the user wants to return to the Option List, the ENTER key must be pressed to continue. In this respect, it is desirable to restrict the number of rooms (and heated spaces) to fourteen so that the entire table can be seen at one time.

Sample Calculation

The data required and the results obtained for a home provide the best illustration of the program. A split-level house sitting on a lot that slopes down to the rear of the house provides several considerations of interest. The floor plan for the house is shown in Fig. 6-2. The rooms and room areas are numbered according to the entry of data in the program. There are four levels in this house, each shifted by an elevation of 4 feet from adjacent levels. The upper two levels, shown in the upper half of the figure, are situated over the lower two levels shown in the lower half of the figure. The living room (room No. 1) is at ground level at the front and the basement (room No. 13) is at ground level in the rear. There is a garage on the west end of the living room level and an open deck on the north side, neither of which are figured into the heat calculations.

The data used in the calculations are listed in Table 6-5. All room size dimensions are entered to the nearest (larger) foot. All window and door sizes are measured to the nearest inch of the sash (excluding trim molding). With the exceptions of the area, wall, and window numbers (columns 2, 4, and 7) the data is entered as shown in the table. Where several values are to be input in one entry, they are separated by commas. Entries that must be entered separately are separated by a slash (/). For the three exceptions mentioned, the maximum number is entered into the program so that the proper number of loops can be executed. For wall, floor, and ceiling insulation input, the program requests the R value of the insulation. The values that were used in the sample calculation are for standard woodframe construction using glass (mineral) wool batts. Table 6-6 summarizes the standard values. If an R value of zero is entered, the program defaults to one of the code tables to let the user make the selection based on construction details. One example of this in the sample data table is shown for the floor in rooms No. 11 and 12 which is an on grade concrete slab having no insulation. After the code of 3 was entered for this construction, the insulation code and thickness were requested. Since there was no insulation, the insulation code for the on grade slab was entered (7) followed with a thickness 0 to satisfy the program requirements. A similar situation exists for the basement level walls.

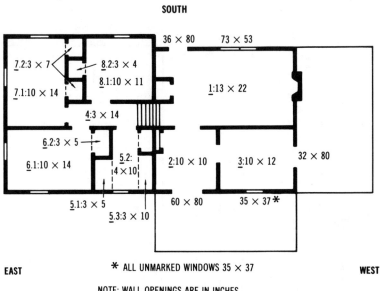

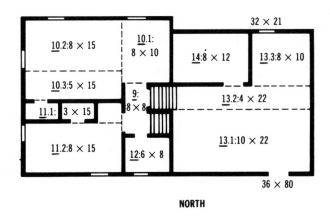

Figure 6-2
Sample house floor plan.

By comparing Fig. 6-2 and Table 6-5, a few additional points may be noted. Data for the floor and ceiling are required only in those cases where they are exposed. The N and Y (no and yes) entries are in response to this inquiry. The upper two levels of the house

Table 6-5. Data for Sample Calculation

Room	Area #	Width/Length	Wall #	Length/Height/Facing	Constr/Insul	Window #	Type/Insul	Width/Height	Floor Type/Insul	Ceiling Type/Insul
1. LIVING	1	13,22	1	22,8,S	1/11.1	1	6/3	36,80		
						2	2/3	73,53		
			2	13,8,W	2/11.1	0			N	Y/1/18.5
2. DINING	1	10,10	1	10,8,N	1/11.1	1	6/3	60,80	N	Y/1/18.5
3. KITCHEN	1	10,12	1	10,8,W	2/11.1	1	6/2	32,80		
			2	12,8,N	1/11.1	1	2/3	35,37	N	Y/1/18.5
4. HALL	1	3,14	1	3,4,W	1/11.1	0			N	Y/1/18.5
5. BATH UP	1	3,5	1	3,8,N	1/11.1	0				Y/1/18.5
	2	4,10	1	4,8,N	1/11.1	1	2/3	35,37	N	Y/1/18.5
	3	3,10	1	3,8,N	1/11.1	0			N	
			2	10,4,W	1/11.1	0			N	Y/1/18.5
6. S BEDRM	1	10,14	1	14,8,N	1/11.1	1	2/3	35,37	N	Y/1/18.5
			2	10,8,E	1/11.1	1	2/3	35,37	N	Y/1/18.5
	2	3,5	0							
7. M BEDRM	1	10,14	1	14,8,E	1/11.1	1	2/3	35,37	N	Y/1/18.5
			2	10,8,S	1/11.1	1	2/3	35,37	N	Y/1/18.5
	2	3,7	1	3,8,S	1/11.1	0				

Room										
8. T BEDRM	1	10,11	1	11,8,S	1/11.1	1	2/3	35,37	N	Y/1/18.5
			2	10,4,W	1/11.1	0				
9. STAIRS	1	8,8	0						Y/4	N
10. REC RM	1	8,10	1	8,4,S	5/5.6	0	2/3	35,37	Y/4	N
			2	8,4,S	3/5.6	1				
	2	8,15	1	23,4,S	5/5.6	0	2/3	35,37	Y/4	N
			2	23,4,S	3/5.6	1				
	3	5,15	1	5,8,E	3/5.6	2	2/3	35,37	Y/4	N
						0			Y/3/7,0	N
11. R BEDRM	1	3,15	1	3,8,E	3/5.6	0	2/3	35,37	Y/3/7,0	N
	2	8,15	1	8,8,E	3/5.6	1	2/3	35,37	Y/3/7,0	N
			2	15,8,N	3/5.6	1				
12. BATH DN	1	6,8	1	8,8,N	3/5.6	1	2/3	35,37	Y/3/7,0	N
13. BASEMNT	1	10,22	1	10,8,W	5/0/1,0	0	6/2	36,80		
			2	22,8,N	4/0/1,0	1			Y/3/7,0	N
			3	10,4,E	5/0/1,0	0			Y/4	N
	2	4,22	1	4,8,W	5/0/1,0	0	2/1	31,21		
	3	8,10	1	10,8,S	5/0/1,0	1			Y/4	N
			2	8,8,W	5/0/1,0	0				
14. STUDY	1	8,12	1	12,8,S	5/0/1,0	0			Y/4	N
			2	8,4,E	5/0/1,0	0				

(rooms 1-8) have exposed ceilings and unexposed floors while for the lower two levels the situation is reversed. A second point should be noted in the wall data for room No. 10, area No. 2. The direction data (N, E, W, S) is used only for reference and is not employed in the calculations. In this instance, in order to save space, the south and east walls were entered together for a total length of 8 + 15 = 23 feet. Since the ground level of the house is about mid-height, the construction codes are different for the upper and lower halves of the walls (3 and 5, respectively). A similar situation can be seen in the basement (room No. 13, area No. 1) where the north wall is exposed, the lower half of the east wall is exposed (5 = below grade) and the upper half is not considered (no data) since it adjoins the recreation room level.

Table 6–6. R Values for Glass Wool Batts

Nominal Thickness (inches)	R Value
1 ½	5.6
2	7.6
4	11.1
6	18.5

Results

As we noted previously, the results of the heat loss calculation can be obtained in nine separate formats. Since the sample house is heated with fuel oil, one of the more useful summaries is in terms of gallons of oil burned per degree day. The reciprocal of this value, that is the number of degree days per gallon of oil, is known as the "k factor." Of course, the k factor obtained from the calculation is an "ideal" value. The summary table is given in Table 6-7. The k factor is 1/0.16 = 6.25 DD/gal. Although actual values might range well in either direction, typical values for homes lie between 4 and 8 DD/gal. In base units of the calculation, this range is respectively 1400-700 BTU/(hr.)(deg).

Data collected (manually) over a three year period for the house used in the calculations are given in Table 6-8. At first glance, the agreement between calculated and measured k factors seems very

Table 6-7. Sample Results in Gal. Fuel Oil/Degree Day

Loss: Room	Total	Ceiling	Walls	Floor	Windows & Doors	Air
LIVING	0.0247	0.0025	0.0030	0	0.0102	0.0090
DINING	0.0103	0.0009	0.0006	0	0.0076	0.0013
KITCHEN	0.0199	0.0010	0.0019	0	0.0094	0.0076
HALL	0.0005	0.0004	0.0001	0	0	0
BATH UP	0.0045	0.0007	0.0013	0	0.0019	0.0005
S BEDRM	0.0107	0.0014	0.0021	0	0.0038	0.0035
M BEDRM	0.0111	0.0014	0.0024	0	0.0038	0.0035
T BEDRM	0.0058	0.0011	0.0014	0	0.0019	0.0014
STAIRS	0.0003	0	0	0.0003	0	0
REC RM	0.0123	0	0.0037	0.0017	0.0057	0.0013
R BEDRM	0.0140	0	0.0037	0.0034	0.0038	0.0030
BATH DN	0.0046	0	0.0011	0.0011	0.0019	0.0006
BASEMNT	0.0394	0	0.0162	0.0038	0.0104	0.0090
STUDY	0.0019	0	0.0014	0.0005	0	0
TOTAL	0.1600	0.0094	0.0389	0.0108	0.0603	0.0407

Table 6-8. Measured Heat Loss for Sample House

Period	Fuel Oil, Gal.	Degree Days Lapsed	k Factor DD/Gal.
12/30/80–2/19/81	304	1764	5.80
12/27/79–2/16/80	309	1897	6.14
12/23/78–2/01/79	212	1304	6.15
Calculated			6.25

impressive. Each period covered the entire month of January (between fuel deliveries) for three successive years. The lower k factor for January 1981 is probably due to decreased efficiency because the oil burner had not been cleaned at the end of the previous heating season. A second factor that works against the 98% agreement between calculated and measured results is that the measured value includes fuel used for heating hot water for domestic use (bath, kitchen, and laundry). An estimate for hot water consumption made on the amount of fuel oil burned during the summer and fall and corrected for the (small) number of degree days yields 0.73 gal/day for domestic hot water. If this correction is applied to the k factor, the three year average becomes 6.90 DD/gal. This result is 10% greater than the calculated value. One possible error in making this correction is that we are overestimating the domestic hot water usage. This is because a certain amount of fuel will be consumed during warm weather just to maintain the water temperature even when hot water is not drawn. During cold weather, the demand for space heating maintains the water temperature and gets figured into the k factor. Unfortunately, how much we have overestimated cannot be calculated for the older data. We can be satisfied, however, that the 10% error is an upper limit. In this single example, at least, our faith in the heat loss calculation is justified.

Numerical Analysis of Data

Chapter 7

Introduction

In Chapter 5, we described several programs for managing the data obtained with the energy monitor interface. For the most part, these programs provide sufficient information to permit you to make changes in energy-consuming habits and improve conservation. In describing the thermometer calibration program, we introduced the practice of curve-fitting data (using the least squares criterion) as a means of summarizing a lot of data in terms of a few coefficients. Finally, the last program described in Chapter 5 provided a means of storing on cassette all of the daily data obtained. In this chapter, we shall discuss some of the statistical techniques that can be used to summarize this data and obtain performance characteristics for the system.

The performance characteristics that we seek will be the coefficients of the least squares curve-fitting equations. It is unlikely that the measurements you make for your house will be identical in all details to those described here. Therefore, you will have to make appropriate modifications to the routines. However, the principles will be the same and we shall use this data for purposes of illustration.

Empirical Relations

Our first task is to establish what relationships exist between the measurements collected. We must identify those measurements that are dependent on others from those that are independent. In all cases, we have to assume the form of the relationship. In equation form, if z is the dependent measurement and y is the independent variable, we can write the relationship as:

$$z = a*y + b$$

The coefficients a and b have to be determined from the z and y data values and are the performance characteristics that describe the relationship. The coefficient a is called the *slope* and measures the extent that z changes for a unit change in y. The coefficient b is called the *intercept* and measures the value of z when y has a value of zero. Alternatively, z may depend linearly on two (or more) independent variables. The general equation in this case is:

$$z = a*y + b*x + c$$

This relationship implies that z is determined by both y and x and that x and y have no dependence on each other. The coefficients a and b are the corresponding slopes and c is the intercept. If we examine what this equation represents in the form of a graph, it is apparent that we require three perpendicular axes or, in other words, a three-dimensional graph. This is illustrated in Fig. 7-1.

Of course, the figure is actually a projection of a three-dimensional surface onto the two dimensions of the page. The y axis appears to be perpendicular to the plane of the page. Only a portion of the surface described by the equation is shown. If x, y, and z can take only positive values, and not negative ones, then the point where all three values are zero (the origin) is the front left corner of a cube whose slope parallel to the front edge (x axis) is equal to the b coefficient, and whose slope parallel to the side edge (y axis) equals the a coefficient. In the figure drawn, the slopes (coefficients) of x and y are 0.25 and 0.5, respectively. For an increase of one unit of x, z will increase by 0.25 unit, while an increase of one unit in y will cause z to increase by 0.5 unit. When x and y are both zero, z will have a value equal to the intercept. In the figure, this is drawn equal to 2 units of z.

If we examine the data collected and stored on cassette tape, we can establish how the entries are related. Recall that the data consists of nine numbers per day saved in a string of from one to

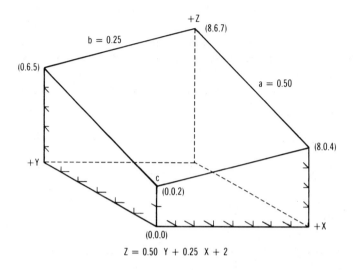

+Z
(8.6.7)

b = 0.25

(0.6.5)

a = 0.50

+Y

(8.0.4)

c
(0.0.2)

(0.0.0)

+X

$$Z = 0.50 \ Y + 0.25 \ X + 2$$

Figure 7-1
Surface of a three-dimensional equation.

five days long with the first entry of the string being the data of the first day. The format of the data strings was shown in Fig. 5-7. Excluding the date, the first seven daily entries are the time-on counts in quarter-minutes for the seven monitoring (set-point) thermometer elements. The remaining two entries are, respectively, the daily outdoor low temperature and high temperature in degrees Fahrenheit. We can label these entries in order as: BATH (B), KITC (K), HOTW (W), LVRM (L), BEDR (S), RECR (R), FURN (F), LO T, and HI T. The high and low daily temperatures are used to calculate the number of degree days which we will label D and create an additional data column. D is obviously an independent variable since it is a measure of how cold it is outdoors and, therefore, related to how much heat would be lost.

Three separate equations can be formulated that relate the amount of heat supplied to each of the three heating zones as a function of the degree days:

$$L = CL*D + DL \qquad (1)$$
$$R = CR*D + DR \qquad (2)$$
$$S = CS*D + DS \qquad (3)$$

We will use two-letter variable names for the coefficients to distinguish them from the data parameters. Coefficients having a C for their first letter will indicate a slope. With the assumption that L, R, and S are independent of each other, equations (1) through (3) can be added together to form one equation:

$$Z = CZ*D + DZ \qquad (4)$$

where Z (for zones) equals L + R + S, then

$$CZ = CL + CR + CS,$$
$$\text{and} \quad DZ = DL + DR + DS.$$

We will want to create an additional data column to store the Z values in order to check the equation (4).

Now, the amount of time that the furnace runs, F, depends on two independent factors: (1) how much heat is supplied to the heating zones, Z, and (2) how much heat is consumed for domestic hot water, W. This is a three-dimensional equation that can be formulated as:

$$F = CW*W + CH*Z + FL \qquad (5)$$

where CH is the coefficient for heating demand, CW is the coefficient for water usage, and the intercept, FL, is the furnace loss; that is, the time the furnace runs to maintain the hot water due to heat loss from the boiler jacket.

The final relationship that can be formulated relates the distribution of domestic hot water between the kitchen and the bathrooms. This equation is:

$$W = CK*K + CB*B + WL \qquad (6)$$

and incorporates an intercept term that accounts for heat loss in this part of the system.

Equations (1) through (6) form the set of equations we can use to evaluate the data collected. Although equations (4) and (6) could be substituted into equation (5) to create one master equation, it becomes somewhat cumbersome. In fact, by limiting each fit to no more than three coefficients to be evaluated, it is possible to use only one (relatively simple) least squares subroutine to separately calculate the coefficients of each equation.

We noted in Chapter 5 the five steps required to generate the set of equations that need to be solved simultaneously in order to calculate the coefficients of the least squares equation. In the applications used there, we were interested in the equation:

$$y = a*x^2 + b*x + c$$

which is a two-dimensional (x and y) and nonlinear (curved due to the x^2 term) function. In the present case, we are interested in both two- (y and z) and three-dimensional (x, y, and z) linear (no squared terms) functions. The most general form of the equation is:

$$z = a*y + b*x + c*w$$

where we introduce the independent variable w for convenience but note that if w is set equal to 1, then the coefficient c will just turn out to be the intercept.

Statistical Preliminaries

Applying the five steps given in Chapter 5, the set of simultaneous equations will be:

$$a*S(y^2) + b*S(xy) + c*S(wy) = S(yz)$$
$$a*S(xy) + b*S(x^2) + c*S(wx) = S(xz)$$
$$a*S(wy) + b*S(wx) + c*S(w^2) = S(wz)$$

where the S( ) terms are the sums taken over, say 15 days, of the squares and products of the measurements being fitted. By using this set of equations is one least squares subroutine, we can avoid having to write six separate least squares routines to analyze the data. For example, equations (5) and (6) can be solved provided we "fake" the data for w by setting all w data values equal to 1. To use this subroutine to solve equations (1) through (4) we set all w values equal to zero and all x values equal to 1. Of course, we still have to assign our real data to the remaining variables and call the subroutine six times but it saves a lot of programming and becomes relatively simple to set up each of the six equations for analysis. To simplify the setups, we can create two additional data table columns, one of which holds all zeros, and one which holds all ones. The one precaution that needs to be taken when the w values are zeroed is to force the $S(w^2)$ term to equal one. This point will be considered further when the BASIC program is described.

Statisticians refer to this calculation as "multiple linear regression analysis." As we have seen previously, there will always be scatter in the data that one obtains in making measurements. It is due to this scatter that we are obliged to seek a "best fit" of the data in the form of an equation and its coefficients. We have also seen that it is desirable to be able to calculate how well the data actually fits the equation. The "goodness of fit" is determined by the magnitude of the root mean square of the residuals known as the "standard error of estimate," or perhaps better called the "residual variance." This quantity gives a measure of the uncertainty (or reliability) of the calculated coefficients. There is another statistical quantity that can be calculated from the residual variance known as the "linear correlation coefficient" and signified by the letter r. The value of r^2 (r-square) is the proportion of the total variance of the dependent variable, z, which is accounted for by the least squares line, $a*y + b$. The linear correlation coefficient (and r-square) takes values between 1 and 0. A value for r-square of 0.28 means that the calculated coefficients account for 28% of the scatter in the data. For one independent variable (y), you can calculate one r-square value. However, when a function has two independent variables (x and y), there are three separate r-square values that can be computed. Technically, these are called "partial" correlation coefficients because each accounts for only 2 of the 3 variables: x and z, y and z, and x and y. For each pair, the third (missing) variable is treated as a constant. As in the two-dimensional case, each r-square can range between 1 (perfect fit) and 0 (no correlation). Of course, if the independent variables, x and y, are truly unrelated, one would hope to find the r-square term close to zero (and the other two values close to one).

The BASIC Program

The Data Numerical Analysis (DNA) program can be divided into three major parts. Line numbers below 1000 are the main program consisting of the initializing and summarizing routine. Line numbers between 1000 and below 2000 form the equation setup subroutine for all six equations to be analyzed. Line numbers in the 2000 range form the generalized least squares subroutine which is called by each of the six equation set-up segments.

The main program is given in Listing 7-1. The program is written to perform the least squares analysis on 15 consecutive days of data in successive increments of 5 days. The 15-day interval was chosen for two reasons. First, it helps to minimize the residual variance by providing a broader data base, and second, 15 rows in the data table displays neatly on the video screen and leaves one display line for column titles. There is nothing sacred about averaging over 15 points in a least squares fit and you may want to try other values to observe the effect. This can be accomplished by changing the initialization value of N in line 100.

The first task of the program is to create a data table (array) having at least 15 rows and 12 columns. Each row holds the data obtained on a particular day. Each column entry in a row contains either a measurement, a value calculated from the measurements, or, in two cases, "dummy" data. Since the data saved on tape comes in blocks consisting of a number of days varying between 1 and 5, the data table must be large enough to accommodate more rows than are needed for the least squares calculations. This is necessary because the cassette read routine expects a complete data string and cannot read a partial data block. As a consequence, the array of data values, V(I,K), is dimensioned to hold 26 rows of 13 columns.

The second task of the program is to fill the data table. A block is read from the cassette tape as a single string (S$) and subsequently

```
100 CLS: CLEAR 500: DIM V(25,13),D(25): I=1: N=15
110 INPUT "LOAD DATA CASSETTE - PRESS PLAY - <ENTER>";X
120 INPUT#-1,S$: S$=S$+" ": X=LEN(S$)
130 W$="": L=0: GOSUB 300
140 X=X-(LEN(W$)+1)
150 D(I)=VAL(W$): PRINT D(I)
160 FOR K=2 TO 10
170 W$="": GOSUB 300
180 V(I,K)=VAL(W$)
190 X=X-(LEN(W$)+1): NEXT K
200 I=I+1: IF X>0 THEN D(I)=D(I-1)+100: PRINT D(I): GOTO 160
210 IF I<21 THEN 120
220 PRINT@960,"PRESS ANY KEY TO START CALCULATIONS AFTER DATA DISPLAYED"
230 W$="######": FOR J=1TO15: PRINTUSINGW$;D(J);
240 FOR K=2TO10
250 PRINTUSINGW$;V(J,K);
260 NEXT K: PRINT: NEXT J
270 PRINT " DATE  BATH  KITC  HOTW  LVRM  BEDR  RECR  FURN  LO T  HI T";
280 W$=INKEY$: IF W$="" THEN 280
290 CLS: GOTO 400
300 L=L+1
310 L$=MID$(S$,L,1)
320 IF L$=" " THEN 350
330 W$=W$+L$
340 GOTO 300
350 RETURN
400 FOR I=1TO25
410 V(I,0)=0: V(I,1)=1
420 V(I,11)=65-((V(I,9)+V(I,10))/2)
430 IF V(I,11)<0 THEN V(I,11)=0
450 V(I,12)=V(I,5)+V(I,6)+V(I,7)
460 NEXT I
470 M=M+1: IF M>10 THEN 600
480 GOSUB 1000
490 INPUT "MORE DATA (Y/N)";A$: IF A$="N" THEN 600
500 FOR I=1TO20: D(I)=D(I+5)
510 FOR K=2TO10: V(I,K)=V(I+5,K)
520 NEXT K: NEXT I
530 I=15
540 IF D(I)=0 THEN 120
550 I=I+1: GOTO 540
600 W$="####.#"
610 PRINT "CW*100: ";: FOR I=1TOM: PRINTUSINGW$;CW(I)*100;: NEXT I: PRINT
620 PRINT "CH*100: ";: FOR I=1TOM: PRINTUSINGW$;CH(I)*100;: NEXT I: PRINT
630 PRINT "FL:     ";: FOR I=1TOM: PRINTUSINGW$;FL(I);: NEXT I: PRINT
640 PRINT "CZ:     ";: FOR I=1TOM: PRINTUSINGW$;CZ(I);: NEXT I: PRINT
650 PRINT "DZ/10:  ";: FOR I=1TOM: PRINTUSINGW$;DZ(I)/10;: NEXT I: PRINT
660 PRINT "CL:     ";: FOR I=1TOM: PRINTUSINGW$;CL(I);: NEXT I: PRINT
670 PRINT "DL/10:  ";: FOR I=1TOM: PRINTUSINGW$;DL(I)/10;: NEXT I: PRINT
680 PRINT "CR:     ";: FOR I=1TOM: PRINTUSINGW$;CR(I);: NEXT I: PRINT
690 PRINT "DR/10:  ";: FOR I=1TOM: PRINTUSINGW$;DR(I)/10;: NEXT I: PRINT
700 PRINT "CS:     ";: FOR I=1TOM: PRINTUSINGW$;CS(I);: NEXT I: PRINT
710 PRINT "DS/10   ";: FOR I=1TOM: PRINTUSINGW$;DS(I)/10;: NEXT I: PRINT
720 PRINT "CK*10:  ";: FOR I=1TOM: PRINTUSINGW$;CK(I)*10;: NEXT I: PRINT
730 PRINT "CB*10:  ";: FOR I=1TOM: PRINTUSINGW$;CB(I)*10;: NEXT I: PRINT
740 PRINT "WL:     ";: FOR I=1TOM: PRINTUSINGW$;WL(I);: NEXT I: PRINT
750 END
```

Listing 7-1. DNA Program, Part 1

stripped one value at a time and loaded into the table. The date associated with each row is stored in a separate list, D(I). Since only the date of the first day in the block is obtained, dates for the subsequent days are calculated by adding 100 to the six digit value: MMDDYY. This creates some interesting looking dates on the display for blocks that overlap the end of a month, such as 103481, but is corrected on following days when the next block is read. As the values for a particular date are stripped from the string, they are assigned to columns No. 2 through No. 10 in the order read. The order in terms of the variable labels is B, K, W, L, S, R, F, Lo T, Hi T, which is the order in which they were recorded on the tape. A space is used to separate the values in the string. The tape read routine continues to read subsequent blocks from the tape until the row index number, I, is equal to or greater than 21. Thus, a minimum of 20 rows will be loaded before the program proceeds to display a table of data covering the first 15 days. The displayed table can be inspected before proceeding. The program is resumed by pressing any key.

The remaining columns of the data table are filled by the loop given in lines 400-460 of the program. The dummy data mentioned above is loaded and consists of a column of zeros in the column having index No. 0, V(I,0), and a column of ones in column No. 1, V(I,1). These are the "data" that are used to fake the least squares subroutine into solving either a two- or three-dimensional equation. Column 11 is the number of degree days calculated from the daily high and low outdoor temperatures stored in columns 9 and 10. These values are processed in lines 430 and 450 of the program including setting all negative values equal to zero. Finally, column 12 is the calculated value for the total zones heat load, Z, obtained by summing L, R, and S (columns 5, 6, and 7).

At this point in the program (line 470), the data table is complete. Because we wish to run the program over more than one 15-day period (advancing in 5-day increments), an index number, M, is incremented: it is initialized to zero by BASIC on the RUN command. M is used to index the coefficients calculated for each 15-day period. In order to display all of the results on the screen at the end of the program, an upper limit of M = 10 is set. This limits the total period spanned by one continuous run of the program to 60 days.

The equation setup subroutine is called at this point (line 480). Before discussing this subroutine, we will examine the rest of the main program. After the calculations have been performed for the current 15-day period, the operator is asked if there is more data available on tape. If there is, the program rebuilds the data table by first shifting the data already resident by five rows and then finding the first empty row down the table. The next block is loaded from tape beginning at this row. It should be noted that row 25 can never be filled and when it is shifted to become row 20, it will set D(20) = 0. When the next block is read from tape it will fill no more than rows 20-24 and still leave row 25 empty.

If there is no more data on tape after the last 15-day period or if 10 periods have been computed, the program concludes by displaying a table of all coefficients for the six equations for each period. The formating and printout of these results are given in lines 600-740. We will discuss the interpretation of the results in the next section.

We now consider the equation set-up subroutine given in Listing 7-2. The subroutine consists of six sections with line numbers for each section occurring in multiples of 100, starting at line 1000. Each section corresponds to one of the empirical equations to be evaluated and is identical in format to the other five. Four pointer variables (P, Q, R, and S) are used to identify the measurements that are to be assigned to the general equation variables (w, x, y, and z, respectively). The first line of each section prints the specific equation. The second line assigns the appropriate column indices to the pointer variables. For example, the first line of the first section (line 1000) prints the specific equation for evaluating the furnace load:

$$F = CW*W + CH*Z + FL$$

If we compare this equation to the general equation:

$$z = a*y + b*x + c*w$$

then z is equivalent to F. The pointer index for z is S and the column index for the furnace, F, is 8; then S = 8. Similarly, with y equivalent to hot water demand, W (column 4), and with x equivalent to zones demand, Z (column 12), the pointer indices will be R = 4 and Q = 12, respectively. Now the intercept FL corresponds to the general coefficient c, so w should be equated to 1. Therefore, the data for w will be from column 1 of the table and P = 1.

```
1000 PRINT "FURNACE LOAD: F = CW*W + CH*Z + FL"
1010 P=1: Q=12: R=4: S=8
1020 GOSUB 2000: IF Y2=0 THEN 1090
1030 CW(M)=A: CH(M)=B: FL(M)=C: PRINT "CW ="CW(M),"CH ="CH(M),"FL ="FL(M)
1040 PRINT "CALCULATED FURNACE DEMAND / MEASURED"
1050 FOR I=1TO20
1060 F=V(I,4)*CW(M)+V(I,12)*CH(M)+FL(M)
1070 PRINT INT(F+0.5)"/"V(I,8),;: NEXT I
1080 PRINT "R↑2 OF W ON F"P2(1),"OF Z ON F"P2(2),"OF W ON Z"P2(3)
1090 INPUT "PRESS <ENTER> TO CONTINUE";A$: CLS
1100 PRINT "DEGREE DAYS VS. HEAT ZONES: Z = CZ*D + DZ"
1110 P=0: Q=1: R=11: S=12
1120 GOSUB 2000: IF Y2=0 THEN 1190
1130 CZ(M)=A: DZ(M)=B: PRINT "CZ ="CZ(M),"DZ ="DZ(M)
1140 PRINT "CALCULATED HEAT ZONES DEMAND / MEASURED"
1150 FOR I=1TO20
1160 Z=CZ(M)*V(I,11)+DZ(M)
1170 PRINT INT(Z+0.5)"/"V(I,12),;
1180 NEXT I
1185 PRINT "R↑2 ="P2(1)
1190 INPUT "PRESS <ENTER> TO CONTINUE";A$: CLS
1200 PRINT "DEGREE DAYS VS. LVRM ZONE: L = CL*D +DL"
1210 P=0: Q=1: R=11: S=5
1220 GOSUB 2000: IF Y2=0 THEN 1290
1230 CL(M)=A: DL(M)=B: PRINT "CL ="CL(M),"DL ="DL(M)
1240 PRINT "CALCULATED LVRM DEMAND / MEASURED"
1250 FOR I=1TO20
1260 Z=CL(M)*V(I,11)+DL(M)
1270 PRINT INT(Z+0.5)"/"V(I,5),;
1280 NEXT I
1285 PRINT "R↑2 ="P2(1)
1290 INPUT "PRESS <ENTER> TO CONTINUE";A$: CLS
1300 PRINT "DEGREE DAYS VS. RECR ZONE: R = CR*D + DR"
1310 P=0: Q=1: R=11: S=7
1320 GOSUB 2000: IF Y2=0 THEN 1390
1330 CR(M)=A: DR(M)=B: PRINT "CR ="CR(M),"DR ="DR(M)
1340 PRINT "CALCULATED RECR DEMAND / MEASURED"
1350 FOR I=1TO20
1360 Z=CR(M)*V(I,11)+DR(M)
1370 PRINT INT(Z+0.5)"/"V(I,7),;
1380 NEXT I
1385 PRINT "R↑2 ="P2(1)
1390 INPUT "PRESS <ENTER> TO CONTINUE";A$: CLS
1400 PRINT "DEGREE DAYS VS. BEDR ZONE: S = CS*D + DS"
1410 P=0: Q=1: R=11: S=6
1420 GOSUB 2000: IF Y2=0 THEN 1490
1430 CS(M)=A: DS(M)=B: PRINT "CS ="CS(M),"DS ="DS(M)
1440 PRINT "CALCULATED BEDR DEMAND / MEASURED"
1450 FOR I=1TO20
1460 Z=CS(M)*V(I,11)+DS(M)
1470 PRINT INT(Z+0.5)"/"V(I,6),;
1480 NEXT I
1485 PRINT "R↑2 ="P2(1)
1490 INPUT "PRESS <ENTER> TO CONTINUE";A$: CLS
1500 PRINT "HOT WATER DISTRIBUTION: W = CK*K + CB*B + WL"
1510 P=1: Q=2: R=3: S=4
1520 GOSUB 2000: IF Y2=0 THEN 1590
1530 CK(M)=A: CB(M)=B: WL(M)=C: PRINT "CK ="CK(M),"CB ="CB(M),"WL ="WL(M)
1540 PRINT "CALCULATED HOT WATER DEMAND / MEASURED"
1550 FOR I=1TO20
1560 Z=(V(I,2)*CB(M))+(V(I,3)*CK(M))+WL(M)
1570 PRINT INT(Z+.5)"/"V(I,4),;: NEXT I
1580 PRINT "R↑2 OF K ON W"P2(1),"OF B ON W"P2(2),"OF K ON B"P2(3)
1590 INPUT "PRESS <ENTER> TO CONTINUE";A$: CLS
1980 RETURN
```

Listing 7-2. DNA Program, Part 2

The only other variation in setting up an equation is for the two-dimensional equations. The second equation in the subroutine is given on line 1100:

$$Z = CZ * D + DZ$$

Comparing this equation to the general equation, we see that with z = Z (column 12) and y = D (column 11) then S = 12 and R = 11. For this case, it is necessary for x = 1 and w = 0 to match the specific equation. Therefore, Q, the index pointer for x, should point to column 1 containing 1s, and P, the index pointer for w, should point to column 0 containing 0s: Q = 1, P = 0. Once the pointer variables have been assigned, the least squares subroutine is called. On return from the subroutine, the coefficients of the specific equation are assigned the values of the corresponding coefficients from the general equation and are listed on the screen.

For the purpose of comparison, the least squares coefficients of the specific equation are then used with the values of the independent variables to calculate the value of the dependent variable. The calculated value and the measured value for a 20-day period are displayed as they are evaluated. Note that we are predicting the last 5 days based on the previous 15 days in this display. Visual comparison of calculated/measured values may not be the most sophisticated statistical calculation but it certainly serves to give the operator a "feel" for the validity of the calculations. After the data is compared, the linear correlation coefficient(s) are listed. This completes this section of the subroutine. The program will proceed to the next section when the ENTER key is pressed.

The last part of the DNA program is the least squares subroutine. This is provided in Listing 7-3. With the exception of the calculation of the linear correlation coefficients, this subroutine uses the same algorithm as the one described in the Thermometer Calibration program in Chapter 5. The sums, S( ), of squares and cross products are collected and assigned to a Z matrix which is then inverted by the subroutine at line 2200. Note the three lines following 2080. The sum of squares of both w and x are set to 1 if they are 0. We noted earlier that this had to be taken care of in the two-dimensional equations for w. The situation with x is in the case when a device did not collect any data. If all 15 y measurements were zero, then Y2 will also be zero and the subroutine is aborted with a "NO CORRELATION" notice printed. The coefficients in this case will be stored as 0s. If these precautions were not taken, the program could abort due to a divide by zero error.

```
2000 REM LEAST SQUARES OF Z = A*Y + B*X + C*W
2010 Y2=0: XY=0: WY=0: X2=0: WX=0: W2=0: WZ=0: XZ=0: YZ=0: Y1=0: X1=0: W1=0:
     Z1=0: Z2=0
2020 FOR I=1TON
2030 Y2=Y2+V(I,R)*V(I,R): XY=XY+V(I,Q)*V(I,R): Y1=Y1+V(I,R)
2040 WY=WY+V(I,P)*V(I,R): X2=X2+V(I,Q)*V(I,Q): X1=X1+V(I,Q)
2050 WX=WX+V(I,P)*V(I,Q): W2=W2+V(I,P)*V(I,P): W1=W1+V(I,P)
2060 WZ=WZ+V(I,P)*V(I,S): XZ=XZ+V(I,Q)*V(I,S): Z1=Z1+V(I,S)
2070 YZ=YZ+V(I,R)*V(I,S): Z2=Z2+V(I,S)*V(I,S)
2080 NEXT I
2082 IF W2=0 THEN W2=1
2084 IF X2=0 THEN X2=1
2086 IF Y2=0 THEN PRINT "NO CORRELATION": RETURN
2090 FOR L=1TO3: FOR C=1TO7: Z(L,C)=0: NEXT C: NEXT L
2100 Z(1,1)=Y2: Z(1,2)=XY: Z(1,3)=WY: Z(1,4)=YZ
2110 Z(2,1)=XY: Z(2,2)=X2: Z(2,3)=WX: Z(2,4)=XZ
2120 Z(3,1)=WY: Z(3,2)=WX: Z(3,3)=W2: Z(3,4)=WZ
2125 FOR I=1TO3: FOR J=1TO4: PRINT Z(I,J),;: NEXT J: NEXT I
2130 FOR C=5TO7: L=C-4: Z(L,C)=1: NEXT C
2135 'FOR L=1TO3: PRINT: FOR C=1TO7: PRINT Z(L,C);: NEXT C: NEXTL
2140 FOR L=1TO3: GOSUB 2200: NEXT L
2145 'FOR L=1TO3: PRINT: FOR C=1TO7: PRINT Z(L,C);: NEXT C: NEXTL
2150 A=Z(1,4): B=Z(2,4): C=Z(3,4)
2155 FOR J=1TO3: R2(J)=0: R1(J)=0: P2(J)=0: NEXT J
2160 R2(1)=(N*YZ-Y1*Z1)↑2/((N*Y2-Y1*Y1)*(N*Z2-Z1*Z1)): R1(1)=SQR(R2(1))
2162 IF W2=1 GOTO 2175
2165 R2(2)=(N*XZ-X1*Z1)↑2/((N*X2-X1*X1)*(N*Z2-Z1*Z1)): R1(2)=SQR(R2(2))
2170 R2(3)=(N*XY-X1*Y1)↑2/((N*X2-X1*X1)*(N*Y2-Y1*Y1)): R1(3)=SQR(R2(3))
2175 P2(1)=(R1(1)-R1(2)*R1(3))↑2/((1-R2(2))*(1-R2(3)))
2180 P2(2)=(R1(2)-R1(1)*R1(3))↑2/((1-R2(1))*(1-R2(3)))
2185 P2(3)=(R1(3)-R1(1)*R1(2))↑2/((1-R2(1))*(1-R2(2)))
2190 RETURN
2200 FOR C=L+1 TO 7: Z(L,C)=Z(L,C)/Z(L,L): NEXT C
2210 Z(L,L)=1
2220 FOR K=1TO3: FOR C=L+1 TO 7
2230 IF K<>L THEN Z(K,C)=Z(K,C)-Z(K,L)*Z(L,C)
2240 NEXT C: NEXT K
2250 FOR K=1TO3
2260 IF K<>L THEN Z(K,L)=0
2270 NEXT K: RETURN
```

Listing 7-3. DNA Program, Part 3

The equations used to calculate the linear correlation coefficients are on lines 2155-2185. Note that the decision to calculate one or three r-square values is based on whether the sum of squares is 1, or not. A sample printout of one 15-day period is presented in Table 7-1.

Table 7–1. Sample Printout of DNA Program Run

DATE	BATH	KITC	HOTW	LVRM	BEDR	RECR	FURN	LO T	HI T
103081	7	710	673	381	0	57	329	43	49
103181	47	511	665	1018	0	369	460	42	49
103281	59	217	425	432	0	167	350	44	59
103381	19	182	564	418	0	143	311	42	64
103481	0	90	462	203	0	58	240	42	66
111181	375	407	775	1448	0	710	535	32	50
111281	40	123	367	1858	51	1187	639	27	48
111381	81	311	633	2040	0	1347	764	23	48
111481	23	90	380	2188	137	1079	566	23	54
111581	80	154	295	1110	0	0	392	34	64
111681	0	217	527	1044	0	0	444	30	54
111781	0	0	0	0	0	0	0	66	66
111881	350	319	597	848	0	933	790	36	49
111981	28	147	617	1183	0	579	641	30	64
112081	47	144	263	1083	0	117	572	28	58

FURNACE LOAD: $F = CW*W + CH*Z + FL$

4.05874E + 06	1.14985E + 07	7243	3.67737E + 06
1.14985E + 07	5.01971E + 07	22188	1.29976E + 07
7243	22188	15	7033

$CW = .312257 \quad CH = .135202 \quad FL = 118.097$

CALCULATED FURNACE DEMAND / MEASURED

387 / 329	513 / 460	332 / 350	370 / 311	298 / 240
652 / 535	651 / 639	774 / 764	697 / 566	360 / 392
424 / 444	118 / 0	545 / 790	549 / 641	362 / 572
1180 / 1512	118 / 0	118 / 0	159 / 99	563 / 739

R 2 OF W ON F .229596   OF Z ON F .633636   OF W ON Z .0614749

DEGREE DAYS VS. HEAT ZONES: $Z = CZ*D + DZ$

6192.5	284	0	520073
284	15	0	22188
0	0	1	0

$CZ = 122.61 \quad DZ = -842.214$

CALCULATED HEAT ZONES DEMAND / MEASURED

1487 / 438	1549 / 1387	813 / 599	629 / 561	506 / 261
2100 / 2158	2530 / 3096	2775 / 3387	2407 / 3404	1120 / 1110
1978 / 1044	− 842 / 0	1917 / 1781	1365 / 1762	1855 / 1200
3633 / 5453	− 842 / 0	− 842 / 0	3143 / 0	3020 / 2126

R 2 = .705464

Table 7-1. Sample Printout of DNA Program Run (cont.)

DEGREE DAYS VS. LVRM ZONE: $L = CL^*D + DL$

6192.5	284	0	350152
284	15	0	15254
0	0	1	0

$CL = 75.2274$ $DL = -407.372$

CALCULATED LVRM DEMAND / MEASURED

1022 / 381	1060 / 1018	608 / 432	495 / 418	420 / 203
1398 / 1448	1661 / 1858	1812 / 2040	1586 / 2188	796 / 1110
1323 / 1044	− 407 / 0	1285 / 848	947 / 1183	1248 / 1083
2338 / 3596	− 407 / 0	− 407 / 0	2038 / 0	1962 / 1000

$R2 = .74634$

DEGREES DAYS VS. RECR ZONE: $R = CR^*D + DR$

6192.5	284	0	164888
284	15	0	6746
0	0	1	0

$CR = 45.5754$ $DR = -413.162$

CALCULATED RECR DEMAND / MEASURED

453 / 57	476 / 369	202 / 167	134 / 143	88 / 58
681 / 710	840 / 1187	931 / 1347	795 / 1079	316 / 0
635 / 0	− 413 / 0	612 / 933	407 / 579	589 / 117
1250 / 1572	− 413 / 0	− 413 / 0	1068 / 0	1022 / 825

$R2 = .51823$

DEGREE DAYS VS. BEDR ZONE: $S = CS^*D + DS$

6192.5	284	0	5033
284	15	0	188
0	0	1	0

$CS = 1.80706$ $DS = -21.6803$

CALCULATED BEDR DEMAND / MEASURED

13 / 0	14 / 0	3 / 0	0 / 0	− 2 / 0
22 / 0	28 / 51	32 / 0	26 / 137	7 / 0
20 / 0	− 22 / 0	19 / 0	11 / 0	18 / 0
44 / 285	− 22 / 0	− 22 / 0	37 / 0	35 / 301

$R2 = .140044$

HOT WATER DISTRIBUTION: $W = CK^*K + CB^*B + WL$

1.35404E + 06	364908	3622	2.12453E + 06
364908	287308	1156	699262
3622	1156	15	7243

$CK = .711098$ $CB = .403975$ $WL = 280.027$

Table 7-1. Sample Printout of DNA Program Run (cont.)

CALCULATED HOT WATER DEMAND / MEASURED				
788 / 673	662 / 665	458 / 425	417 / 564	344 / 462
721 / 775	384 / 367	534 / 633	353 / 380	422 / 295
434 / 527	280 / 0	648 / 597	396 / 617	401 / 263
658 / 1039	280 / 0	280 / 0	363 / 132	383 / 504
R 2 OF K ON W .485246		OF B ON W .111728		OF K ON B 1.99849E − 03

Interpretation of Results

A few words of caution are in order at the outset. If you have little
or no experience with experimental measurements, your first
impression of the calculated results may be disappointing. You
have to remember the limitations of the measurements set the
limits of the results. For instance, the set-point devices measure
the time that hot water was drawn through the pipes. Although the
set point was adjusted as shown in Fig. 5-2, the assumption
implicit in measuring time as a measure of heat consumption is
that the water flow rate is always the same. Now this assumption
is probably adequate in the case of the heat zones where (for the
system described) one circulating pump drives all three zones.
However, for the hot water drawn for domestic use, the flow rate
is determined by each faucet adjustment. As a consequence, we
would expect more uncertainty in the CW coefficient. The only
way that this problem could be solved would be to use flow
meters. Unfortunately, flow meters that are suitable for
interfacing are very expensive to purchase and to install. For our
purposes, the time measurement provides sufficient information
about the system as long as not too much is expected in the
precision of the data. The calculated coefficients are a satisfactory
way to summarize and compare a lot of data that would otherwise
be too unmanageable to give much information. However, for all
the statistical calculations that can be made, there is no substitute
for common sense when it comes to interpreting results. We might
also add that there is nothing so humbling to theoretical
expectations as experimental results.

There are other precautions that should be noted. One, in
particular, is the assumption of independence of variables. Our

calculations make this assumption, for example, regarding the three heat zones. Much to the author's chagrin and well into the data collection, it was found that the L heat zone valve does not always seat properly and that when the R zone valve opened, the circulator pump pulled enough hot water through the L valve to trigger its set-point thermometer occasionally. Even more importantly, with one circulator driving all three zones, the flow rate would be less when two or three zones are on simultaneously. In principal, cross product terms such as $CC*L*R$, etc., would have to be added into the empirical least squares equations. In practice, this is probably more detail than is desired given the limitations already noted for the sensors.

Turning now to an examination of the sample data shown in Fig. 7-1, it should be noted that the printout was obtained by changing most of the PRINT statements in the DNA program to LPRINTS plus some minor modifications in the print formatting. Since our assumption has been that a line printer is not attached to the computer, each section in Table 7-1 separated by space represents one screen display. Advancing to each subsequent section requires the operator to press the ENTER key.

After the program has read in sufficient data blocks to fill the data table, the first 15 days (rows) of the table (including the dates) are displayed. The data table shown in Table 7-1 illustrates several problems. Since the date of the first data block on tape was 103081 and it was a 5-day block, the four subsequent dates are calculated and range up to 103481. Of course, this date is actually 110381. The next block should have begun with 110481 except that a power failure resulted in the loss of 7 days, data from 110481 through 111081. This is a minor disaster that cannot be easily avoided. It does not, however, significantly affect the calculations to omit missing data since each day's measurements do not depend on any other day's measurements. As long as the missing data does not span a period during which significant changes in the heating system occurred, the calculations can be expected to be acceptable. The disadvantage is that the record of degree days will be in error when the amount of fuel consumed over the period is used to evaluate the k factor described in Chapter 6. A second power failure on 111781 resulted in the loss of one day's measurements. In this instance, the data tables in the computer were rebuilt from written records. Zeros were entered for all time-on values and, note particularly, the high and low outdoor temperatures were entered as 66°F to yield a D (degree day value) of zero.

The six displays following the data display correspond to each of the six equations that is evaluated. Each screen display follows the same format. The first line consists of the title and equation. This is followed by the 3-row by 4-column "Z matrix" of sums, of the general form:

$$S(Y2) \quad S(XY) \quad S(WY) \quad S(YZ)$$
$$S(XY) \quad S(X2) \quad S(WX) \quad S(XZ)$$
$$S(WY) \quad S(WX) \quad S(W2) \quad S(WZ)$$

Note that either S(X2) or S(W2) will be equal to 15 (the number of data summed) for the two- or three-dimensional equations, respectively. The first three columns of the matrix are symmetric with respect to the rows, with the entry in the first row, second column identical to the entry in the second row, first column, etc. The line following the matrix lists the calculated values of the coefficients of the equation. All of the values displayed to this point are printed to 6-digit significance. Although this is far too many digits for the precision warranted for the coefficients, we will reserve rounding off to 4-digit significance in the final summary table.

The second to last part of the screen display consists of the comparison of the calculated and measured values of the dependent variable (the term on the left-hand side of the equation). The measured values come directly from the appropriate column (and row) of the data table. The calculated values are obtained by evaluating the right-hand side of the equation by multiplying each of the slope coefficients by the corresponding data table entry and adding these to the intercept value. These values are rounded off to integer values in agreement with the measured values. Note, in particular, that negative values may be calculated. This is not an error in the calculations. Typically, negative values will occur when the measured value is zero. Since our measurements can only be made over the positive range it might seem appropriate to convert all negative values to zero. This was not done because it hides relevant features of the equation.

The last line displayed lists the r-square values. As discussed previously, these give a statistical measure of the fit of the data to the equation. The interpretation of these values comes with experience. For the applications described here, a rough guide is that r-square values greater than 80% are very good, between 50% and 80% are fair, between 10% and 50% are poor, and below 10% indicate no correlation. Arguments could be made on either side that these guidelines are too strict or too lenient. You can form your own opinion best by weighing the r-square value against the list of calculated/measured values.

A few specific comments about the calculations in Table 7-1 might clear up some details. Consider the first equation which evaluates the furnace demand. The coefficient CW = 0.31 means that (on the average) for every quarter-minute that hot water is drawn, the furnace will have to run for 0.31 quarter-minutes. Actually, the units of time do not have to be in quarter-minutes, they may be any unit as long as the same unit is applied to both measurements. Thus the coefficient CH = 0.135 can be interpreted that for every 100 minutes that heat is supplied to one or more zones, the furnace will run for 13.5 minutes, etc. The intercept value, FL = 118, means that (again on the average) the furnace will run a total of about 30 minutes (118/4) per day whether heating or hot water demands are made or not. Based on data obtained during the summer months it was observed that the furnace ran about 25 quarter-minutes once every fourth hour. This would equal 150 quarter-minutes per day in reasonable agreement with the calculated intercept. The r-square values appear reasonable (although better values have been obtained in other periods). R-square for W on Z is somewhat high.

In examining the coefficients of the three zone demand equations, excellent agreement is obtained between the three separate zones (L, R, and S) and the total (Z). In each case, the slope coefficient is the number of quarter-minutes that heat is supplied to each zone in a 24-hour period for each degree day of that period. Both sums, CL + CR + CS and DL + DR + DS, equal CZ and DZ, respectively, to five digits. The intercepts of all four equations are negative. At first glance, this might seem contradictory. However, a better interpretation is obtained by evaluating the alternate intercept on the D axis rather than the intercepts on the zone axis of the equations. For example, in the L zone equation:

$$L = CL*D + DL$$

DL is the value of L when D is zero. The alternate intercept is the value of D when L is zero. This is obtained algebraically as:

$$D(L = 0) = -(DL/CL)$$

The value obtained is the number of degree days that must occur before a demand for heat is made in the zone. For this 15-day period, the values for the three zones are: $D(L = 0) = 5.4$; $D(R = 0) = 9.1$; and $D(S = 0) = 12.0$. These values are related to the thermostat settings in the zones. The thermostat settings for L, R, and S were approximately 68, 65, and 60°F, respectively. The poor fit of the S zone can be attributed to the scant data obtained over the period.

The last equation to be interpreted is the domestic hot water distribution. It has already been observed that this fit would be expected to be the poorest because of erratic flow rates. The fact that r-square for the kitchen demand is close to 50% is probably because the largest demand is made by an automatic dishwasher that draws water at a consistent rate. The near zero (r-square) correlation between kitchen and baths is gratifying.

After the results of the sixth equation have been displayed for the last 15-day period, either because 10 periods (60 days) have been processed, or because there is no more data on tape, a summary listing of all coefficients is displayed. A sample of this display is shown in Table 7-2. The left-hand column lists the particular coefficients scaled so that they are printed in the format XXX.X. The purpose was to have most of the numbers lie between 10 and 100 but maintain consistency for similar coefficients. Thus the zone intercepts (DZ, DL, DR, and DS) have been divided by 10, the furnace slopes (CW and CH) have been multiplied by 100, and the water distribution slopes (CK and CB) have been multiplied by 10. This means that the actual value for CW listed in the first row and first column is 0.152 (15.2/100). The reason for formatting the coefficients is to emphasize that, in general, only the digits to the left of the decimal point are meaningful (significant).

Table 7-2. Sample Printout of DNA Summary Table

CW*100:	15.2	7.7	24.8	31.2	61.7	30.1	30.0	8.7	-1.2	28.7
CH*10:	16.4	16.2	13.7	13.5	13.2	22.1	16.7	18.6	21.2	19.5
FL:	117.0	173.6	104.4	118.1	26.6	76.3	124.2	198.9	187.5	130.4
CZ:	103.8	105.8	145.0	122.6	93.0	69.7	77.8	43.9	77.8	91.0
DZ/10:	-74.6	-73.4	-124.1	-84.2	-15.0	5.3	-2.0	80.8	2.5	-12.3
CL:	69.7	70.5	87.9	75.2	56.9	43.8	53.6	29.7	38.7	49.1
DL/10:	-50.0	-47.1	-67.9	-40.7	-1.4	2.0	-9.5	46.2	27.3	-8.8
CR:	33.9	35.2	55.2	45.6	31.6	22.5	21.8	14.4	39.0	41.9
DR/10:	-25.1	-27.0	-54.9	-41.3	-9.5	6.0	9.0	32.8	-24.7	-3.5
CS:	0.2	0.1	1.9	1.8	4.5	3.5	2.4	-0.3	0.0	0.0
DS/10:	0.6	0.6	-1.2	-2.2	-4.1	-2.7	-1.6	1.8	0.0	-0.0
CK*10:	6.1	4.2	6.2	7.1	21.4	17.9	14.7	12.3	15.3	10.6
CB*10:	22.8	9.7	5.2	4.0	-4.2	-3.3	12.6	15.4	4.2	4.7
WL:	339.3	418.0	318.2	280.0	63.2	141.7	196.9	246.6	213.7	280.5

Each column of coefficients corresponds to one 15-day period. The first period evaluated is on the left. As a point of reference, the data listed in Table 7-1 is summarized in the fourth column (from the left). Actually, for this program run, only the columns 1–4 should be considered valid. The remaining columns (5–10) were included to emphasize one very important point. During the period beginning on 112381 (column 5) a wood stove heater was operated in the L zone (recall that a large part of the load for the S zone was shown to be carried by the L zone in the system). Because a set-point thermometer was NOT used to monitor the wood stove, the remaining heat load data is not valid. The erratic values for the coefficients in columns 5–10 verify this fact. Columns 5–7 cover the period of "mixed" data obtained both before and after the wood stove was put into use. It was hoped that once the wood stove contribution covered an entire period (column 8 and later) that the coefficients would stabilize. This apparently is not the case. The important lesson to be learned is that all sources of heat must be monitored in order to obtain reasonable results.

We conclude by noting that the coefficients have been kept in units of time. In principle, one could calculate the amount of fuel consumed per unit of time and, assuming a value for the heat content of the fuel (such as used in the program given in Chapter 6), the energy (BTU) equivalent coefficients for F could be determined. If you should be interested in making this conversion, bear in mind that the efficiency of the burner will be figured into your results. Efficiencies for oil burners around 83% are considered very good. Manufacturer's ratings in terms of maximum fuel consumption and BTU/hr ratings should be attached to the unit.

Summary

1. A program to process energy-monitor data read from cassette tape is described.
2. The processing consists of the least squares evaluation of the coefficients of two- and three-dimensional heat balance equations.

3. The values of the coefficients indicate the current (average) performance of energy consumption and distribution in the residence.
4. The long-term trend of the coefficients indicates changes (improvement or deterioration) of the energy efficiency.

Postscript: The Next Byte

After your system is operational and you have analyzed sufficient data to know its performance characteristics, you will most likely want to study other energy sources and drains. One important feature of energy monitoring is that temperature measurements have many applications because some of the energy is always ultimately converted (degraded) into heat. The system, as developed, offers many measurement opportunities. The frequency/timer transducers can be used with other sensors that depend on either an electrical resistance or (more rarely) a capacitance. As you purchase mail order electronic supplies, you will start to receive the supplier's catalogs. Study the catalogs for components that are possible solutions to your applications.

Besides the on-board capabilities of your system, you can add additional boards in parallel to the 44-pad edge connector of the MIDAS bus. Additional boards can be other I/O ports or memory registers. Recall that the bus is active for output all the time and will be activated for input for device codes below 128 and memory addresses above 32K. One of the weakest features of most systems is their dependence on house power. A crashed system due to power failure means that some data is irretreivably lost. If 2 Kbytes of read/write memory were added that had battery backup, the TNT monitor and data storage tables could be relocated (after recompiling the routine) in a less vulnerable environment.

Other energy related data acquisition will undoubtedly be of interest to some readers. Items that come to mind include solar and wind (and weather) monitors. In addition to temperature sensors already in the system, there are various transducers available on the hobbyist market that are easily interfaced through an input port. Do not overlook the simplicity of single-bit (flag) transducers. Besides the 555 timer that functions as a one-bit analog to digital (time pulse) converter, there are many applications that are inherently digital: that is, off or on. For example, the light-emitting diode (LED) or any other lamp as a signal source can be used with a photodiode or phototransistor functioning as a detector. If you read the various popular electronics and computer magazines, you will find many hints for solving your interfacing problems.

The one final topic that must be mentioned concerns the area of microcomputer interfacing applications for control of external devices. If (or when) you undertake this exciting area of computer interfacing, arm yourself with a lot of reading, studying, and experimenting. It may be trite but you must remember that a computer can only do what it is told to do. Not only must you anticipate every conceivable way your system can fail but you must reckon with all of the consequences of failure. Failsafe systems have to allow for not only the possibility of power failure but also for what will happen when the power is restored to the device before the computer's program is restored. DO NOT override discrete failsafe devices already built into the devices that you want to incorporate into your computer system. For control applications, there are devices that can make simple ON/OFF control (solid-state relays) and proportional control (silicon controlled rectifiers) of high power devices (up to 15 amperes at 120 volts) with single-bit digital level signals.

One specific energy control project you may consider is summer cooling by controlling attic fans as the temperature rises above a set point. Another project that might prove useful is valve (or pump) control for solar hot water heaters. If you do get into a project that is more than turning on and off passive devices, such as motor or valve control, see what is available in industrial controls for homes at plumbing supply houses.

You should be familiar with opto-isolation devices before you tackle any project that uses electrical power from any other source than your interface power supply. Finally, always allow for manual override in any system that involves computer control.

Component List

Appendix A

Quantity	Reference	Description	Source*
		INTEGRATED CIRCUITS	
1	IC11	7400 Quad 2-In NAND Gate	
2	IC5,6	7402 Quad 2-In NOR Gate	
2	IC8,13	7432 Quad 2-In OR Gate	
1	IC12	7474 Dual D Flip-Flop	
2	IC19,20	74125 Quad 3-State Inverter	
1	IC7	74LS138 3-to-8 Line Decoder	
1	IC17	74148 Priority Encoder	
4	IC1,2,9,10	74365 Hex 3-State Buffer	
2	IC14,16	8216 Bidirectional Bus Driver	
1	IC15	NSC5309 Clock Circuit	(Jameco)
4	IC21-24	555 Dual Timers	
		PASSIVE ELEMENTS	
4	R1-4	7.5K, ½ watt Resistor	
11	R5-7,9-16	10K, ¼ watt Resistor	
1	R8	100K, ¼ watt Resistor	
8	C1-8,17-20	1.0 μF, 35 V Tantalum Capacitors	
12	C9-16	0.01 μF, 25 V Disc Capacitors	
1	Q1	2N3905 Transistor	(Jameco)
33	D1,QDT1-8	1N914 Diodes (1N4148 equivalent)	
1	TX1	16 V, 30 mA Sec. Clock Transformer	(Jameco)

Appendix A (cont.)

HARDWARE

100		Vector T44 Wirewrap Posts	
18	AC1-2,T1-16	AP Single row, Rt. angle Male Headers	
20	X1-40	AP Double row, Rt. angle Male Headers	
3	S1-3	Panasonic Momentary Switch	(Digi-Key)
13	-	14-pin Wirewrap Sockets	
13	-	16-pin Wirewrap Sockets	
1	-	28-pin Wirewrap Sockets	
3	IC18,25,26	16-pin DIP Header Plugs	

MISCELLANEOUS

1	Vector P3662 4½ × 6½" Wirewrap Board
1	Modified Wrap Wirewrap Tool
1	50 ft. Spool 30 ga. Wirewrap Wire
8	50 ft. Spool 26 ga. Multistrand Wire
1	TRS-80 type 40-Conductor Cable
1	+5 V, ±12 V Power Supply (see text)

POSSIBLE MAIL ORDER SUPPLIERS (*Source listed if only one of the following suppliers stocks the item):

Digi-Key Corp.
P.O. Box 677
Thief River Falls, MN 56701

Jameco Electronics
1355 Shoreway Dr.
Belmont, CA 94002

Priority One Electronics
16723 Roscoe Blvd.
Sepulveda, CA 91343

```
                    00100 ;EXTERNAL CLOCK DRIVEN THERMOMETER MONITOR
                    00110 ;COPYRIGHT 1981 BY PAUL E. FIELD
0072                00120 BASIC    EQU     0072H
3C3F                00130 VIDEO    EQU     3C3FH
7A5B                00140          ORG     7A5BH
7A5B D300           00150 CLKEN    OUT     (0),A
7A5D DB00           00160          IN      A,(0)
7A5F E670           00170          AND     70H
7A61 FE00           00180          CP      0
7A63 C25B7A         00190          JP      NZ,CLKEN
7A66 3EC3           00200          LD      A,0C3H       ;LOAD JUMP AT RST7
7A68 321240         00210          LD      (4012H),A
7A6B 21777A         00220          LD      HL,SCAN
7A6E 221340         00230          LD      (4013H),HL
7A71 ED56           00240          IM      1
7A73 FB             00250          EI
7A74 C37200         00260          JP      BASIC
7A77 F5             00270 SCAN     PUSH    AF
7A78 C5             00280          PUSH    BC
7A79 D5             00290          PUSH    DE
7A7A E5             00300          PUSH    HL
7A7B CDE57A         00310          CALL    CLOCK
7A7E 7E             00320          LD      A,(HL)
7A7F FE30           00330          CP      '0'
7A81 2B             00340          DEC     HL
7A82 CA987A         00350          JP      Z,HALF
7A85 FE35           00360          CP      '5'
7A87 C2DF7A         00370          JP      NZ,NONE
7A8A 7E             00380          LD      A,(HL)
7A8B FE31           00390          CP      '1'
7A8D CAA37A         00400          JP      Z,TIME
7A90 FE34           00410          CP      '4'
7A92 CAA37A         00420          JP      Z,TIME
7A95 C3DF7A         00430          JP      NONE
7A98 7E             00440 HALF     LD      A,(HL)
7A99 FE33           00450          CP      '3'
7A9B CAA37A         00460          JP      Z,TIME
7A9E FE30           00470          CP      '0'
7AA0 C2DF7A         00480          JP      NZ,NONE
7AA3 CD067B         00490 TIME     CALL    TEMP      ;ON RET: HL=MBHT(HR),BC=MBCT
7AA6 E5             00500          PUSH    HL        ;AND D=HR DISP.  SAVE MBHT
7AA7 213F3C         00510          LD      HL,VIDEO  ;S1
7AAA 97             00520          SUB     A
7AAB 5F             00530          LD      E,A
7AAC 7E             00540          LD      A,(HL)
7AAD E60F           00550          AND     0FH
7AAF 83             00560          ADD     A,E
7AB0 5F             00570          LD      E,A
7AB1 2B             00580          DEC     HL
7AB2 7E             00590          LD      A,(HL)    ;S10
7AB3 E60F           00600          AND     0FH
7AB5 83             00610          ADD     A,E
7AB6 5F             00620          LD      E,A
7AB7 2B             00630          DEC     HL
7AB8 2B             00640          DEC     HL
```

Assembler Listing of TNT Monitor

```
7AB9 7E        00650          LD A,(HL)        ;S1
7ABA E60F      00660          AND 0FH
7ABC 83        00670          ADD A,E
5ABD 5F        00680          LD E,A
7ABE 2B        00690          DEC HL
7ABF 7E        00700          LD A,(HL)        ;M10
7AC0 E60F      00710          AND 0FH
7AC2 83        00720          ADD A,E
7AC3 C2DE7A    00730          JP NZ,DONE
7AC6 5F        00740          LD E,A
7AC7 2B        00750          DEC HL
7AC8 2B        00760          DEC HL
7AC9 7E        00770          LD A,(HL)        ;H1
7ACA E60F      00780          AND 0FH
7ACC 83        00790          ADD A,E
7ACD 5F        00800          LD E,A
7ACE 2B        00810          DEC HL
7ACF 7E        00820          LD A,(HL)        ;H10
7AD0 E60F      00830          AND 0FH
7AD2 83        00840          ADD A,E
7AD3 C5        00850          PUSH BC
7AD4 D5        00860          PUSH DE
7AD5 CCFD7B    00870          CALL Z,DAY
7AD8 D1        00880          POP DE           ;D=HR. DISPLACEMENT
7AD9 C1        00890          POP BC           ;(BC)=MBCT
7ADA E3        00900          EX (SP),HL       ;(HL)=MBHT
7ADB CDDC7B    00910          CALL HOUR
7ADE E1        00920 DONE     POP HL
7ADF E1        00930 NONE     POP HL
7AE0 D1        00940          POP DE
7AE1 C1        00950          POP BC
7AE2 F1        00960          POP AF
7AE3 FB        00970          EI
7AE4 C9        00980          RET
7AE5 213F3C    00990 CLOCK    LD HL,VIDEO      ;S1
7AE8 D300      01000          OUT (0),A
7AEA DB00      01010          IN A,(0)
7AEC 4F        01020          LD C,A
7AED E670      01030          AND 70H
7AEF 07        01040          RLCA
7AF0 07        01050          RLCA
7AF1 07        01060          RLCA
7AF2 07        01070          RLCA
7AF3 2F        01080          CPL
7AF4 3C        01090          INC A
7AF5 85        01100          ADD A,L
7AF6 6F        01110          LD L,A
7AF7 79        01120          LD A,C
7AF8 E60F      01130          AND 0FH
7AFA C630      01140          ADD A,30H
7AFC 77        01150          LD (HL),A
7AFD 7D        01160          LD A,L
7AFE FE3F      01170          CP VIDEO&0FFH    ;LOW VIDEO ADDR.
7B00 C2E57A    01180          JP NZ,CLOCK
7B03 DB00      01190          IN A,(0)
```

Assembler Listing of TNT Monitor (cont.)

```
7B05  C9         01200         RET
7B06  01A87C     01210  TEMP   LD BC,BASE
7B09  1600       01220         LD D,0
7B0B  21383C     01230         LD HL,VIDEO-7    ;H10
7B0E  7E         01240         LD A,(HL)
7B0F  E60F       01250         AND 15
7B11  FE00       01260         CP 0
7B13  CA227B     01270         JP Z,ONE
7B16  FE01       01280         CP 1
7B18  CA207B     01290         JP Z,TEN
7B1B  1614       01300         LD D,20
7B1D  C3227B     01310         JP ONE
7B20  160A       01320  TEN    LD D,10
7B22  23         01330  ONE    INC HL
7B23  7E         01340         LD A,(HL)
7B24  E60F       01350         AND 15
7B26  C602       01360         ADD A,2
7B28  82         01370         ADD A,D
7B29  57         01380         LD D,A           ;D=HOUR DISPLACEMENT
7B2A  D5         01390  PREP   PUSH DE
7B2B  C5         01400         PUSH BC
7B2C  110000     01410         LD DE,0
7B2F  21907C     01420         LD HL,BUF
7B32  D301       01430         OUT (1),A
7B34  0EFF       01440         LD C,0FFH
7B36  13         01450  COUNT  INC DE
7B37  DB01       01460         IN A,(1)
7B39  A9         01470         XOR C
7B3A  CA367B     01480         JP Z,COUNT
7B3D  77         01490         LD (HL),A
7B3E  23         01500         INC HL
7B3F  47         01510         LD B,A
7B40  79         01520         LD A,C
7B41  2F         01530         CPL
7B42  A8         01540         XOR B
7B43  2F         01550         CPL
7B44  4F         01560         LD C,A
7B45  73         01570         LD (HL),E
7B46  23         01580         INC HL
7B47  72         01590         LD (HL),D
7B48  23         01600         INC HL
7B49  97         01610         SUB A
7B4A  81         01620         ADD A,C
7B4B  13         01630         INC DE
7B4C  13         01640         INC DE
7B4D  13         01650         INC DE
7B4E  C2367B     01660         JP NZ,COUNT
7B51  C1         01670         POP BC
7B52  D1         01680         POP DE
7B53  1E80       01690         LD E,128
7B55  21907C     01700  DEVNO  LD HL,BUF
7B58  7E         01710  TEST   LD A,(HL)
7B59  23         01720         INC HL
7B5A  23         01730         INC HL
7B5B  23         01740         INC HL
```

Assembler Listing of TNT Monitor (cont.)

```
7B5C A3       01750          AND  E
7B5D CA587B   01760          JP  Z,TEST
7B60 L5       01770          PUSH DE
7B61 2B       01780          DEC HL
7B62 56       01790          LD  D,(HL)
7B63 2B       01800          DEC HL
7B64 5E       01810          LD  E,(HL)
7B65 EB       01820          EX  DE,HL
7B66 D1       01830          POP DE
7B67 7B       01840          LD  A,E
7B68 3D       01850          DEC A
7B69 CA957B   01860          JP  Z,THERM
7B6C C5       01870          PUSH BC
7B6D 03       01880          INC BC
7B6E 0A       01890          LD  A,(BC)      ;MBSP
7B6F BC       01900          CP  H
7B70 DA867B   01910          JP  C,NEXT
7B73 0B       01920          DEC BC
7B74 C27C7B   01930          JP  NZ,TALLY
7B77 0A       01940          LD  A,(BC)      ;LBSP
7B78 BD       01950          CP  L
7B79 DA867B   01960          JP  C,NEXT
7B7C 79       01970 TALLY    LD  A,C
7B7D 82       01980          ADD A,D
7B7E 4F       01990          LD  C,A
7B7F D2837B   02000          JP  NC,SKIP1
7B82 04       02010          INC B
7B83 0A       02020 SKIP1    LD  A,(BC)
7B84 3C       02030          INC A
7B85 02       02040          LD  (BC),A
7B86 C1       02050 NEXT     POP BC
7B87 3E1A     02060          LD  A,26
7B89 81       02070          ADD A,C
7B8A D28E7B   02080          JP  NC,SKIP2
7B8D 04       02090          INC B
7B8E 4F       02100 SKIP2    LD  C,A
7B8F 7B       02110          LD  A,E
7B90 0F       02120          RRCA
7B91 5F       02130          LD  E,A
7B92 C3557B   02140          JP  DEVNO
7B95 7D       02150 THERM    LD  A,L
7B96 02       02160          LD  (BC),A      ;BC=CURRENT TEMP. PTR.
7B97 03       02170          INC BC
7B98 7C       02180          LD  A,H
7B99 02       02190          LD  (BC),A
7B9A 7A       02200          LD  A,D         ;GET HOUR DISP.
7B9B D602     02210          SUB 2
7B9D 07       02220          RLCA            ;MULTIPLY BY 4
7B9E 07       02230          RLCA
7B9F C602     02240          ADD A,2
7BA1 81       02250          ADD A,C
7BA2 6F       02260 LOCK     LD  L,A
7BA3 60       02270          LD  H,B
7BA4 D2A87B   02280          JP  NC,SKIP3
7BA7 24       02290          INC H
```

Assembler Listing of TNT Monitor (cont.)

```
7BA8 0A       02300 SKIP3   LD A,(BC)        ;GET MBYTE OF C.T.
7BA9 BE       02310         CP (HL)          ;MBLT(HR)
7BAA DAB97B   02320         JP C,HICK
7BAD C2D17B   02330         JP NZ,LXC
7BB0 2B       02340         DEC HL
7BB1 0B       02350         DEC BC
7BB2 0A       02360         LD A,(BC)
7BB3 BE       02370         CP (HL)          ;LBLT(HR)
7BB4 23       02380         INC HL
7BB5 03       02390         INC BC
7BB6 D2D17B   02400         JP NC,LXC
7BB9 23       02410 HICK    INC HL
7BBA 23       02420         INC HL
7BBB 0A       02430         LD A,(BC)
7BBC BE       02440         CP (HL)          ;MBHT(HR)
7BBD DAC87B   02450         JP C,HXC
7BC0 C0       02460         RET NZ
7BC1 2B       02470         DEC HL
7BC2 0B       02480         DEC BC
7BC3 0A       02490         LD A,(BC)
7BC4 BE       02500         CP (HL)          ;LBHT(HR)
7BC5 23       02510         INC HL
7BC6 03       02520         INC BC
7BC7 D0       02530         RET NC
7BC8 0A       02540 HXC     LD A,(BC)
7BC9 77       02550         LD (HL),A
7BCA 2B       02560         DEC HL
7BCB 0B       02570         DEC BC
7BCC 0A       02580         LD A,(BC)
7BCD 77       02590         LD (HL),A
7BCE 23       02600         INC HL
7BCF 03       02610         INC BC
7BD0 C9       02620         RET
7BD1 0A       02630 LXC     LD A,(BC)
7BD2 77       02640         LD (HL),A        ;MBLT(HR)
7BD3 2B       02650         DEC HL
7BD4 0B       02660         DEC BC
7BD5 0A       02670         LD A,(BC)
7BD6 77       02680         LD (HL),A        ;LBLT(HR)
7BD7 03       02690         INC BC
7BD8 23       02700         INC HL
7BD9 23       02710         INC HL
7BDA 23       02720         INC HL           ;MBHT(HR)
7BDB C9       02730         RET
7BDC 0A       02740 HOUR    LD A,(BC)        ;MBCT
7BDD 77       02750         LD (HL),A        ;MBHT(HR)
7BDE 2B       02760         DEC HL
7BDF 2B       02770         DEC HL
7BE0 77       02780         LD (HL),A        ;MBLT(HR)
7BE1 0B       02790         DEC BC
7BE2 23       02800         INC HL
7BE3 0A       02810         LD A,(BC)        ;LBCT
7BE4 77       02820         LD (HL),A        ;LBHT(HR)
7BE5 2B       02830         DEC HL
7BE6 2B       02840         DEC HL
```

Assembler Listing of TNT Monitor (cont.)

```
7BE7 77        02850        LD  (HL),A        ;LBLT(HR)
7BE8 01A87C    02860        LD  BC,BASE
7BEB 1E07      02870        LD  E,7
7BED 7A        02880        LD  A,D
7BEE 81        02890 AGAIN  ADD A,C
7BEF D2F37B    02900        JP  NC,SKIP
7BF2 04        02910        INC B
7BF3 4F        02920 SKIP   LD  C,A
7BF4 97        02930        SUB A
7BF5 02        02940        LD  (BC),A
7BF6 1D        02950        DEC E
7BF7 C8        02960        RET Z
7BF8 3E1A      02970        LD  A,26
7BFA C3EE7B    02980        JP  AGAIN
7BFD 21FF7F    02990 DAY    LD  HL,MTOP
7C00 01ED7F    03000        LD  BC,MTOP-18
7C03 112E02    03010        LD  DE,558
7C06 0A        03020 MORE   LD  A,(BC)        ;ADVANCE DAY RECORDS
7C07 77        03030        LD  (HL),A
7C08 0B        03040        DEC BC
7C09 2B        03050        DEC HL
7C0A 1B        03060        DEC DE
7C0B 7B        03070        LD  A,E
7C0C B2        03080        OR  D
7C0D C2067C    03090        JP  NZ,MORE
7C10 21607D    03100        LD  HL,CTEMP+2
7C13 4E        03110        LD  C,(HL)        ;=LBLT(H0)
0C14 23        03120        INC HL
7C15 46        03130        LD  B,(HL)        ;=MBLT(H0)
7C16 23        03140        INC HL
7C17 5E        03150        LD  E,(HL)        ;=LBHT(H0)
7C18 23        03160        INC HL
7C19 56        03170        LD  D,(HL)        ;=MBHT(H0)
7C1A 3E17      03180        LD  A,23
7C1C F5        03190 REPT   PUSH AF           ;SAVE COUNT
7C1D 23        03200        INC HL
7C1E 23        03210        INC HL
7C1F 7E        03220 LCHK   LD  A,(HL)        ;=MBLT(HN)
7C20 B8        03230        CP  B
7C21 DA347C    03240        JP  C,HCHK
7C24 C22E7C    03250        JP  NZ,LEX
7C27 2B        03260        DEC HL
7C28 7E        03270        LD  A,(HL)        ;=LBLT(HN)
7C29 B9        03280        CP  C
7C2A 23        03290        INC HL
7C2B DA347C    03300        JP  C,HCHK
7C2E 7E        03310 LEX    LD  A,(HL)
7C2F 47        03320        LD  B,A           ;=MBLT(HN)
7C30 2B        03330        DEC HL
7C31 7E        03340        LD  A,(HL)        ;=LBLT(HN)
7C32 4F        03350        LD  C,A
7C33 23        03360        INC HL            ;(MBLT(HN))
7C34 23        03370 HCHK   INC HL
7C35 23        03380        INC HL
7C36 7E        03390        LD  A,(HL)        ;=MBHT(HN)
```

Assembler Listing of TNT Monitor (cont.)

```
7C37 BA        03400        CP  D
7C38 DA457C    03410        JP  C,HEX
7C3B C24B7C    03420        JP  NZ,TCHK
7C3E 2B        03430        DEC HL
7C3F 7E        03440        LD  A,(HL)      ;=LBHT(HN)
7C40 BB        03450        CP  E
7C41 23        03460        INC HL          ; (MBHT(HN))
7C42 D24B7C    03470        JP  NC,TCHK
7C45 7E        03480 HEX    LD  A,(HL)
7C46 57        03490        LD  D,A         ;=MBHT(HN)
7C47 2B        03500        DEC HL
7C48 7E        03510        LD  A,(HL)
7C49 5F        03520        LD  E,A         ;=LBHT(HN)
7C4A 23        03530        INC HL
7C4B F1        03540 TCHK   POP AF
7C4C 3D        03550        DEC A
7C4D C21C7C    03560        JP  NZ,REPT
7C50 3E0F      03570        LD  A,15
7C52 85        03580        ADD A,L
7C53 6F        03590        LD  L,A
7C54 D2587C    03600        JP  NC,SKIP4
7C57 24        03610        INC H
7C58 71        03620 SKIP4  LD  (HL),C
7C59 23        03630        INC HL
7C5A 70        03640        LD  (HL),B
7C5B 23        03650        INC HL
7C5C 73        03660        LD  (HL),E
7C5D 23        03670        INC HL
7C5E 72        03680        LD  (HL),D
7C5F 21A87C    03690        LD  HL,BASE     ;SUM SET POINT TIMES
7C62 0607      03700        LD  B,7
7C64 23        03710 SETP   INC HL
7C65 23        03720        INC HL
7C66 0E18      03730        LD  C,24
7C68 110000    03740        LD  DE,0
7C6B 7E        03750 LOOP   LD  A,(HL)
7C6C 83        03760        ADD A,E
7C6D 5F        03770        LD  E,A
7C6E D2727C    03780        JP  NC,OVER
7C71 14        03790        INC D
7C72 23        03800 OVER   INC HL
7C73 0D        03810        DEC C
7C74 C26B7C    03820        JP  NZ,LOOP
7C77 E5        03830        PUSH HL
7C78 21CE7D    03840        LD  HL,TDAY
7C7B 7D        03850        LD  A,L
7C7C 90        03860        SUB B
7C7D D2817C    03870        JP  NC,JMP1
7C80 25        03880        DEC H
7C81 90        03890 JMP1   SUB B
7C82 D2867C    03900        JP  NC,JMP2
7C85 25        03910        DEC H
7C86 6F        03920 JMP2   LD  L,A
7C87 73        03930        LD  (HL),E
7C88 23        03940        INC HL
```

Assembler Listing of TNT Monitor (cont.)

```
7C89 72      03950           LD (HL),D
7C8A E1      03960           POP HL
7C8B 05      03970           DEC B
7C8C C2647C  03980           JP NZ,SETP
7C8F C9      03990           RET
0018         04000 BUF       DEFS 24
00B6         04010 BASE      DEFS 182
0061         04020 CTEMP     DEFS 97
000F         04030 DTOP      DEFS 15
0231         04040 TDAY      DEFS 561
0001         04050 MTOP      DEFS 1
0000         04060           END
00000 TOTAL ERRORS
```

DTOP	7DBF	SKIP1	7B83
JMP2	7C86	TALLY	7B7C
JMP1	7C81	NEXT	7B86
TDAY	7DCE	THERM	7B95
OVER	7C72	TEST	7B58
LOOP	7C6B	DEVNO	7B55
SETP	7C64	COUNT	7B36
SKIP4	7C58	BUF	7C90
TCHK	7C4B	PREP	7B2A
HEX	7C45	TEN	7B20
LEX	7C2E	ONE	7B22
HCHK	7C34	BASE	7CA8
LCHK	7C1F	HOUR	7BDC
REPT	7C1C	DAY	7BFD
CTEMP	7D5E	DONE	7ADE
MORE	7C06	TEMP	7B06
MTOP	7FFF	TIME	7AA3
SKIP	7BF3	NONE	7ADF
AGAIN	7BEE	HALF	7A98
HXC	7BC8	CLOCK	7AE5
LXC	7BD1	SCAN	7A77
HICK	7BB9	CLKEN	7A5B
SKIP3	7BA8	VIDEO	3C3F
LOCK	7BA2	BASIC	0072
SKIP2	7B8E		

Assembler Listing of TNT Monitor (cont.)

Appendix C

```
100 CLEAR 150: CLS: PRINT@207,"RESIDENTIAL HEAT LOSS CALCULATIONS": DEFINT I,N
110 PRINT: INPUT "HOW MANY ROOMS AND HEATED SPACES";NR
120 DIM Q(7),R(12),U(6,3),RM$(NR),LT(NR),LI(NR),LP(NR),LW(NR),LC(NR),LF(NR),CC(4),F
    C(4),RW(4),RL(4),NP(4),PA(4,4),PL(4,4),PH(4,4),PD$(4,4),PC(4,4),PU(4,4),NW(4,4)
    ,WA(4,4),WS(4,4)
125 FOR I=1 TO 6: FOR J=1 TO 3: READ U(I,J): NEXT J: NEXT I
130 FOR I=1 TO 12: READ R(I): NEXT I
135 FOR I=1 TO 7: READ Q(I): NEXT I
140 FOR I=1 TO NR: CLS: PRINT "NAME OF ROOM #";I;: INPUT RM$(I)
145 LP(I)=0: LW(I)=0: LI(I)=0: LF(I)=0: LC(I)=0
150 INPUT "HOW MANY RECTANGULAR AREAS IN THIS ROOM";NA
160 FOR J=1 TO NA: PRINT@128,CHR$(31);
170 PRINT"ENTER 'WIDTH(FT), LENGTH(FT)' OF "RM$(I);" AREA #";J;
180 INPUT RW(J),RL(J)
190 INPUT "HOW MANY EXPOSED WALLS IN THIS AREA";NP(J)
200 IF NP(J)=0 GOTO 460 ELSE AF=0
210 FOR K=1 TO NP(J): PRINT@256,CHR$(31);
215 PRINT"'LENGTH(FT),HEIGHT(FT),DIRECTION(N/S/E/W)' OF WALL #";K;
220 INPUT PL(J,K),PH(J,K),PD$(J,K)
230 X$=PD$(J,K): GOSUB 1000
240 PRINT@832,"WALL CONSTRUCTION: 1=WOODFRAME,SIDING  2=WOODFRAME,UNSHEATHED"
250 PRINT TAB(19);"3=MASONRY,FURRED     4=MASONRY,PLAIN"
260 PRINT TAB(19);"5=BELOW GRADE(.18";CHR$(34);")";
270 PRINT@320,"";: INPUT "WALL CONSTRUCTION CODE";PC(J,K)
275 IF PC(J,K)=2 OR PC(J,K)=4 THEN AF=2.5
280 PC(J,K)=R(PC(J,K))
285 INPUT "ENTER INSULATION R-VALUE (IF NOT KNOWN ENTER 0)";RV
290 IF RV=0 GOSUB 1050
300 PU(J,K)=1/(PC(J,K)+RV)
305 WA(J,K)=0: WS(J,K)=0
310 PRINT@320,CHR$(31);: PRINT "ENTER NUMBER OF WINDOWS PLUS DOORS IN ";X$;" WALL
    OF AREA";J;: INPUT NW(J,K)
320 IF NW(J,K)=0 THEN WA(J,K)=0: GOTO 440
325 FOR L=1 TO NW(J,K)
330 PRINT@832,"TYPE: 1=CASED WINDOW( <0.75CFM)  2=CASED WINDOW"
335 PRINT"      3=FIXED/PICTURE          4=JALOUSIE"
340 PRINT"      5=SLIDING GLASS DOORS    6=OTHER DOOR";
345 PRINT@384,"";: INPUT "ENTER TYPE CODE";IC
350 IF IC=6 GOSUB 1150 ELSE GOSUB 1200
390 INPUT "ENTER 'WIDTH(INCHES),HEIGHT(INCHES)'";W,H
400 AW=W*H/144: WA(J,K)=WA(J,K)+AW
410 WL=AW*U(IC,IT): WS(J,K)=WS(J,K)+WL
430 PRINT@384,CHR$(31);: NEXT L
440 PA(J,K)=(PL(J,K)*PH(J,K))-WA(J,K)
450 LP(I)=LP(I)+(PU(J,K)*PA(J,K))
455 LW(I)=LW(I)+WS(J,K): NEXT K
460 PRINT@192,CHR$(31);: PRINT "IS "RM$(I)" AREA #"J" OVER UNHEATED SPACE";: INPUT Q$
470 IF LEFT$(Q$,1)="N" THEN 550
480 PRINT@832,"FLOOR TYPE: 1=OVER CLOSED SPACE  2=OVER VENTED SPACE/GARAGE"
490 PRINT TAB(12);"3=ON GRADE SLAB      4=BELOW GRADE SLAB ( >18";CHR$(34);")";
500 PRINT@256,"";: INPUT "ENTER 'FLOOR CODE'";FC(J)
505 IF FC(J)=4 THEN RV=0: GOTO 540
```

BASIC Program Listing for Residential Heat Loss

171

```
510 IF FC(J)=3 THEN PF=0: GOSUB 1130: GOTO 550
520 INPUT "ENTER INSULATION R-VALUE (IF NOT KNOWN ENTER 0)";RV
530 IF RV=0 GOSUB 1050
540 LF(I)=LF(I)+(RW(J)*RL(J))/(RV+R(FC(J)+5))
550 PRINT@256,CHR$(31);: PRINT"IS "RM$(I)" AREA #"J" UNDER  UNHEATED SPACE";: INPUT Q$
560 IF LEFT$(Q$,1)="N" THEN 645
570 PRINT@832,"CEILING TYPE: 1=UNDER VENTED ROOF/SPACE"
580 PRINT"              2=EXPOSED BEAMS OR RAFTERS"
590 PRINT"              3=COMBINED ROOF-CEILING";
600 PRINT@320,"";: INPUT "ENTER 'CEILING CODE'";CC(J)
610 INPUT "ENTER INSULATION R-VALUE (IF NOT KNOWN ENTER 0)";RV
620 IF RV=0 GOSUB 1050
630 IF CC(J)>1 GOSUB 1100 ELSE CW=RW(J)
640 LC(I)=LC(I)+(CW*RL(J))/(RV+R(CC(J)+9))
645 IF NP(J)=0 GOTO 670
650 AN=0: FOR K=1 TO NP(J)
655 IF NW(J,K)>0 THEN AN=AN+1: L=K
660 NEXT K
665 LI(I)=LI(I)+(0.009*AN*RW(J)*RL(J)*PH(J,L)*AF)
670 NEXT J: NEXT I
690 CLS: PRINT@256,"SUMMARY LISTING:     /DEGREE DAY     /HOUR"
700 PRINT "  ENERGY   (BTU)        1            6"
705 PRINT "  FUEL OIL (gAL)        2            7"
710 PRINT "  NAT. GAS (SCF)        3            8"
715 PRINT "  ELECTRIC (KWH)        4            9"
720 PRINT "  PER CENT              5": PRINT "  QUIT";TAB(40)"0"
725 PRINT: INPUT "ENTER SUMMARY CODE";Q
730 IF Q<6 GOTO 745
735 INPUT "ENTER AVERAGE OUTDOOR TEMPERATURE (DEG. F)";OT
740 INPUT "            DESIRED INDOOR TEMPERATURE (DEG. F)";TI
745 ON Q GOTO 755,760,765,770,775,780,785,790,795
750 END
755 Z=1/24: A$="#########": GOTO 800
760 Z=137000/24: A$="####.####": GOTO 800
765 Z=1050/24: A$="######.##": GOTO 800
770 Z=3412/24: A$="######.##": GOTO 800
775 Z=1: A$="######.##": GOTO 800
780 Z=1/(TI-OT): A$="#########": GOTO 800
785 Z=137000/(TI-OT): A$="####.####": GOTO 800
790 Z=1050/(TI-OT): A$="######.##": GOTO 800
795 Z=3412/(TI-OT): A$="######.##"
800 CLS: PRINT "ROOM/LOSS:   TOTAL  CEILING    WALLS    FLOOR WINDOWS&DOORS AIR
    "
810 FOR I=1 TO NR: LT(I)=LC(I)+LP(I)+LF(I)+LW(I)+LI(I)
815 IF Z=1 AND I=1 THEN GOSUB 950
820 PRINT RM$(I);TAB(9);: PRINTUSINGA$;LT(I)/Z;LC(I)/Z;LP(I)/Z;LF(I)/Z;LW(I)/Z;LI(I)/Z
830 IF I<14 AND I<>NR THEN NEXT I
840 GOSUB 910: NEXT I
850 S=0: FOR I=1 TO NR: S=S+(LT(I)/Z): NEXT I
855 PRINT "TOTALS = ";: PRINTUSINGA$;S;
860 S=0: FOR I=1 TO NR: S=S+(LC(I)/Z): NEXT I
865 PRINTUSINGA$;S;
870 S=0: FOR I=1 TO NR: S=S+(LP(I)/Z): NEXT I
875 PRINTUSINGA$;S;
880 S=0: FOR I=1 TO NR: S=S+(LF(I)/Z): NEXT I
885 PRINTUSINGA$;S;
890 S=0: FOR I=1 TO NR: S=S+(LW(I)/Z): NEXT I
```

BASIC Program Listing for Residential Heat Loss (Cont.)

Appendix C (cont.)

```
895 PRINTUSINGA$;S;
900 S=0: FOR I=1 TO NR: S=S+(LI(I)/Z): NEXT I
905 PRINTUSINGA$;S;: INPUT Q: GOTO 690
910 ON Q GOTO 911,912,913,914,915,916,917,918,919
911 PRINT "BTU/DEGREE DAY"TAB(60);: INPUT Q: RETURN
912 PRINT "GAL OIL/DEGREE DAY"TAB(60);: INPUT Q: RETURN
913 PRINT "SCF GAS/DEGREE DAY"TAB(60);: INPUT Q: RETURN
914 PRINT "KWH/DEGREE DAY"TAB(60);: INPUT Q: RETURN
915 PRINT "PER CENT/DEGREE DAY"TAB(60);: INPUT Q: RETURN
916 PRINT "BTU/HOUR"TAB(60);: INPUT Q: RETURN
917 PRINT "GAL OIL/HOUR"TAB(60);: INPUT Q: RETURN
918 PRINT "SCF GAS/HOUR"TAB(60);: INPUT Q: RETURN
919 PRINT "KWH/HOUR"TAB(60);: INPUT Q: RETURN
950 Z=0: FOR J=1 TO NR: Z=Z+LT(J): NEXT J
960 Z=Z/100: RETURN
970 DATA 1.50,0.95,0.90,2.55,2.05,1.20,1.40,0.85,0.85,7.50,7.50,2.20,2.50
    ,2.00,2.00,4.50,2.40,1.30
980 DATA 3.57,1.50,3.33,2.08,16.5,7.14,3.57,1.33,33.3,1.53,3.22,3.22
990 DATA 3.70,3.33,5.88,4.55,3.45,2.77,0.33
1000 IF X$="N" THEN X$="NORTH"
1010 IF X$="S" THEN X$="SOUTH"
1020 IF X$="E" THEN X$="EAST"
1030 IF X$="W" THEN X$="WEST"
1040 RETURN
1050 PRINT@832,CHR$(31);"FIBER INSULATION: 1=BLANKET/BATT      2=LOOSE/BLOWN"
1060 PRINT"EXPANDED TYPES:   3=URETHANE    4=RUBBER      5=STYRENE/OTHER"
1070 PRINT"SPECIAL TYPES:    6=ROOF DECK SLAB   7=FLOOR SLAB PERIMETER";: PRINT@44
     8,"";
1075 INPUT "ENTER 'TYPE CODE, THICKNESS(INCHES)'";C,T
1080 RV=Q(C)*T: RETURN
1100 INPUT "ENTER 'MAXIMUM HEIGHT,MINIMUM HEIGHT'";X,Y
1110 CW=SQR((RW(J)+2)+(X-Y)+2)
1120 RETURN
1130 FOR K=1 TO NP(J)
1135 IF PC(J,K)<>16.5 THEN PF=PF+PL(J,K)
1140 NEXT K: GOSUB 1050
1145 LF(I)=LF(I)+PF/(RV+R(FC(J)+5)): RETURN
1150 PRINT@832,CHR$(31);: PRINT "INSULATION:  1=NONE"
1160 PRINT "              2=WEATHER STRIPPING OR STORM DOOR (NOT BOTH)"
1170 PRINT "              3=BOTH WEATHER STRIPPING AND STORM DOOR";: PRINT@448,"";
1175 INPUT "ENTER INSULATION CODE";IT
1180 IF IT=1 AND AF=0 THEN AF=2
1185 IF AF=0 THEN AF=1
1190 RETURN
1200 PRINT@832,CHR$(31);: PRINT "CLASS:· 1=SINGLE GLASS"
1210 PRINT "        2=DOUBLE GLASS"
1220 PRINT "        3=STORM SASH";: PRINT@448,"";
1230 INPUT "ENTER CLASS CODE";IT
1240 IF IT=1 AND AF=0 THEN AF=2
1245 IF AF=0 THEN AF=1
1250 RETURN
```

BASIC Program Listing for Residential Heat Loss (Cont.)

Notes

Notes

Index

Index

READER SERVICE CARD

To better serve you, the reader, please take a moment to fill out this card, or a copy of it, for us. Not only will you be kept up to date on the Blacksburg Series books, but as an extra bonus, **we will randomly select five cards every month, from all of the cards sent to us during the previous month. The names that are drawn will win, absolutely free, a book from the Blacksburg Continuing Education Series.** Therefore, make sure to indicate your choice in the space provided below. For a complete listing of all the books to choose from, refer to the inside front cover of this book. Please, one card per person. Give everyone a chance.

In order to find out who has won a book in your area, call (703) 953-1861 anytime during the night or weekend. When you do call, an answering machine will let you know the monthly winners. Too good to be true? Just give us a call. Good luck.

If I win, please send me a copy of:

_____

I understand that this book will be sent to me absolutely free, if my card is selected.

For our information, how about telling us a little about yourself. We are interested in your occupation, how and where you normally purchase books and the books that you would like to see in the Blacksburg Series. We are also interested in finding authors for the series, so if you have a book idea, write to The Blacksburg Group, Inc., P.O. Box 242, Blacksburg, VA 24060 and ask for an Author Packet. We are also interested in TRS-80, APPLE, OSI and PET BASIC programs.

My occupation is _____

I buy books through/from _____

Would you buy books through the mail? _____

I'd like to see a book about _____

Name _____

Address _____

City _____

State _____ Zip _____

MAIL TO: BOOKS, BOX 715, BLACKSBURG, VA 24060
!!!!!PLEASE PRINT!!!!!